C000193163

UNMASKING AND DEFEATING DEMONS

150 QUESTIONS AND ANSWERS ABOUT DEMONS AND EVIL SPIRITS (DEMON ATTACK, SPIRITUAL WARFARE, DEMONIC POSSESSION, DEMONIC COVENANTS AND CURSES, DEMONIC DELIVERANCE)

REV. EZEKIEL KING

Copyright 2019 @ Rev. Ezekiel King

Rev. Ezekiel King

FOREWORD

The information contained in this book is completely true and accurate facts of life and spirituality. No aspect may be regarded as fiction or fabrication, and as such, may be acted upon accordingly.

3

Rev. Ezekiel King

DISCLAIMER

In this book is to be found quotations from the Holy Bible, a book freely available to the world and so all such quotations are outside the author's rights of ownership to this book.

Also to be found herein are some quotations from popular religious figures, all of who lived and died in times before the 20th century of our present era. Credits have been given where due and the author of this book does not lay claim to any of these quotations.

These distinguished figures of the past quoted herein include St. Augustine (15th Century AD), Sun Tzu (545 BC–470 BC) and King James of England Scotland (14th century) all of whom authored works that are to be found in the public domain today.

All other quotations herein are either that of the author or extracts from his other books.

Rev. Ezekiel King

POINT OF NOTE

The questions in this book are not arranged in alphabetical order, but according to an order best suited to spiritual need and curiosity. To find a specific question, please go through the **Table of Content** and pick the one you want.

Rev. Ezekiel King

TABLE OF CONTENT

Rev. Ezekiel King

7

Rev. Ezekiel King

9

11

Rev. Ezekiel King

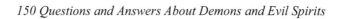

13

Rev. Ezekiel King

UNDERSTANDING HUMANITY'S ENEMY

Ever since the creation of the earth, there has been a group of powerful supernatural beings who are completely dedicated to the destruction of all that which the living God, the creator of all things, loves. Of all His creations, it is not the moon, not the sun or the stars, it is not the mighty universe, the solar system or the planets in it, but mortal man, he is the one God cherishes above all. Hence, mankind is the prime target of these powerful supernatural beings who are collectively known as demons or evil spirits, entities of utter evil.

Unfortunately, man knows none of these things. He does not understand God's great love for him and the great danger he faces because of that. Even where he senses that danger he has no idea how to avoid or defeat it. He doesn't know that there are some very powerful weapons and abilities God has given him for free to defeat every possible danger or evil. In his ignorance, man blunders from life into death and takes his children with him all the way.

Rev. Ezekiel King

6 My people are destroyed for lack of knowledge: because thou hast rejected knowledge, I will also reject thee, that thou shalt be no priest to me: seeing thou hast forgotten the law of thy God, I will also forget thy children.

Hosea 4:6 King James Version (KJV-)

Hosea was one of the minor prophets of ancient Israel who spoke to the people with the voice of God during the reign of King Jeroboam II (c. 786–746 BC). This was a time when Israel was deep in sin and rejected by God, much like the world is today. Hosea authored the book of prophecies that bears his name.

A prophet is a man specially chosen by God, usually before birth, and sent as a messenger or a worker of authority unto the world. People like these are extremely rare. Every true prophet has a unique task or

15

message particular to his time and is
divinely blessed with the abilities
necessary to accomplish it all,
beginning at a certain age (usually
30 or 40).

The most basic ability a
prophet possesses is that of spiritual
vision (the ability to see and hear
supernatural or spiritual things of all
kinds). On the other hand, not all
who are blessed with this basic ability
are prophets. Some are even evil and
others just frauds.

The author of this book you
are reading is a prophet of God.

The message Hosea had for the world was simple. Man does not know his God and creator or his true enemy. He lacks knowledge about the terrible war being waged against him and the only one who can save him, and for this, he suffers.

Even today, mankind has not bettered himself in wisdom. His ignorance of the existence of demons and evil

Rev. Ezekiel King

spirits is staggering, the same invincible entities that are his worst enemy, his sworn enemy!

For those who know very little or nothing about demons and evil spirits, their evil works and ways; unto you have I written this book. That you may understand, unmask and defeat your enemy once and forever.

One of the wisest men ever to walk the earth was Sun Tzu, a great thinker and a military general who lived in the ancient lands of China a few centuries after Hosea's time and he has this to say about defeating one's enemy...

> *The key to victory in war is to*
> *understand your enemy. His strategy*
> *and his thinking; his weapons and*
> *his actions.*
>
> **Sun Tzu (The Art of War)*

As you can see from the quotation above, a seasoned military general believes that victory against one's enemy lies, not in the strength of his army, but in understanding his enemy completely. This is total knowledge of his enemy's nature, actions, strength, and weakness.

17

This book is a collection of all the questions anyone can ever ask about demons and evil spirits, spoken or thought. In-depth answers are given to every single question and explanation is done in detail. I have poured out my knowledge, decades of experience, and God-given wisdom in this book and even tapped from other events in history to ensure that my message gets through to every mind. The information accumulated herein will raise your understanding of the activities of these demons and evil spirits from 0 to 100%.

Reading this book, you will come to understand that your hateful neighbor, that betraying relative, spouse or child, the offending friend or colleague, the criminals and vile people of this world that attack you for no reason, none of them qualify as your worst enemy. Instead, you should be very wary of the invincible evil beings, who attack people in mysterious ways and even use them as tools to destroy the lives of others. These are the worst enemies of mankind and that includes you!

By the knowledge in this book, you will learn to understand, unmask and defeat these evil beings in order to set yourself free forever.

Rev. Ezekiel King

1. WHAT ARE DEMONS?

Demons are extremely evil entities or spirits (supernatural beings) whose primary objective is to harm human beings. They are very terrifying to humans and that fear gives them more power. Exorcism and consecrations are thought to be the best ways to get rid of them under any circumstance, but what people do not understand is that demons vary in strength, rank, and abilities. While consecration and exorcism work effectively to get rid of certain lesser demons, it does not work that easily for powerful, high-ranking demons, some of whom can harm a priest or a man of God directly; the priests of the early Catholic church discovered this fact the hard way.

Interestingly, a Franciscan friar of the time named Ludovico Maria Sinistrari stated clearly that Incubi demons "do not obey exorcists, have no dread of exorcisms, show no reverence for holy things, at the approach of which they are not in the least overawed"

19

Rev. Ezekiel King

*Total Deliverance Form
Spiritual Husband and Spiritual
Wife: Incubus and Succumbs,
Incubus Demons… published by Rev.
Ezekiel King.

If left unchecked, the presence of a demon in a house, around or inside a person can lead to serious injury, disaster or even death.

Demons can confuse a man and lead him in the wrong path. He will end up doing things he normally wouldn't do and cannot explain what came over him during the actions.

Demons, being spirits and pure evil in nature, are generally referred to as **evil spirits** because there are a lot of other good spirits such as angels and the spirits of dead loved ones. One popular name for demons among humans, however, is based on that of their leader Satan, the devil, "the evil one", hence they are often referred to as satanic spirits or devilish spirits. To Christians, demons are also known as the "legions of Lucifer", or "fallen angels". They were with Lucifer, the chief angel, in the day he rebelled against his God and was cast out of heaven. From then on, they became the servants of Lucifer, who became known as Satan, *Satanhan* or the Chief fallen angel, the devil.

Answer 2

Modern scientific and intellectual response to the question of demons leaves no room for their existence. For worldly people, God, angels, demons, and all other spirits, simply do not exist outside the imagination of fools and Hollywood movies. And this is what Hosea and a host of other prophets have been warning about since ancient times; mankind rejecting knowledge about his existence.

Below is a standard response of modern man to the issue of the existence of demons and you will come across it in many advanced level books including textbooks, dictionaries, and encyclopedias…

In the mythology of most cultures, demons appear as personifications of evil supernatural powers. In their efforts to limit, control and understand the supernatural and natural forces, powers and enemies at work in their lives, ancient peoples (and even modern people who reject rational thought) adopt beliefs in demons. Demons are

21

Rev. Ezekiel King

delusions and have no reality, whatever, outside the imagination of individuals who believe in them. However, to those individuals, the demons can be perfectly real and quite harmful.

Answer 3

Demons: Singular form of demons. A single evil entity or a fallen angel. Also called an evil spirit.

Answer 4

Demons are evil entities of the dark world who wander the earth tormenting humans.

Rev. Ezekiel King

2. DO DEMONS REALLY EXIST?

According to Christianity and the Holy Bible, demons are fallen angels. They were originally full-fledged angelic beings in heaven who jointly opposed God at a time that was just after the creation of the earth and before the creation of humanity. Hence, they were stripped of their holiness and cast out of heaven, down unto the earth. Thus, they became demons, evil entities of darkness.

Demons are fallen angels. They are here on earth but on a different plane of existence. Hence, we cannot see or sense them. They hate humans as much as humans are loved by God and will do them great harm at every opportunity. They cause humans all manner of pain, unhappiness, sickness, and destruction.

Rev. Ezekiel King

Demons, like angels, are powerful supernatural beings that cannot be seen by ordinary human eyes, hence mankind has always doubted their existence since ancient times. With the advent of science and technology to explain a lot of puzzling things about nature, that doubt is a lot stronger now than ever.

But do these evil beings really exist? Yes, they defiantly do!

One of the most striking proofs of the personal existence of Satan, which our times afford us, is found in the fact, that he has so influenced the minds of multitudes in reference to his existence and doings, as to make them believe that he does not exist; and that the hosts of Demons or Evil Spirits, over whom Satan presides as Prince, are only the fantasies of the brain, some hallucination of the mind. Could we have a stronger proof of the existence

Rev. Ezekiel King

*of a mind so mighty as to produce
such results?*

**Spiritualism, a Satanic
Delusion, and a Sign of the Times"
published in 1856by Pastor William
Ramsey.*

In that way that man, centuries ago when he couldn't see them with his naked eyes, doubted and denied the existence of microscopic organisms such as bacteria and other disease causing germs, and minute particles such as atoms and electrons, until the invention of the microscope allowed him to see them, so also does he doubt and deny the existence of supernatural beings which includes demons.

Since ancient times, people have told tales of encountering demons, incidents of demonic possessions, manifestations and strange occurrences. In the most spectacular cases, cults and pagan religions have been known to arise; this is where people end up creating images, shrines, and idols in the worship of demons.

25

Those who worship idols and pagan gods are really worshipping and sacrificing to demons. Demons live to deceive people into worshipping themselves (1 Corinthians 10:20-21).

****

10 Let no one be found among you who sacrifices their son or daughter in the fire, who practices divination or sorcery, interprets omens, engages in witchcraft, 11 or casts spells, or who is a medium or spiritist or who consults the dead. 12 Anyone who does these things is detestable to the Lord; because of these same detestable practices the Lord your God will drive out those nations before you. 13 You must be blameless before the Lord your God.

Rev. Ezekiel King

Deuteronomy 18:10-13 New
International Version (NIV)

Man has actually known about demons for a very long time. He has worshiped and communicated with them in different ways over the ages and that is one reason the living God is so far from humanity and the world today. Hence, everything is in chaos.

Answer 2

According to modern science and other related studies, demons are merely a figment of the imagination that leads to fear, anger and negative thoughts, each of which can do more harm than good.

Bottom line, demons do not exist and people are simply fooling themselves by believing differently!

Answer 3

Rev. Ezekiel King

Many learned people believe that certain hard drugs, such as cocaine, crystal meth, weed, and heroin, can induce hallucinations, so deep it causes one to image demons and creepy beings of all kinds.

The reality here that many do not understand is that these drugs, which are addictive, lays waste to every defensive mechanism in the human body and soul, making a person the perfect host for demons (demonic possession).

Unfortunately, most people do not believe in demons and so view people in this situation as just being under the influence of hard drugs. They try to treat them in light, but always fail.

Answer 4

At a time after the creation of angels, and certainly, after the sixth day of creation of the earth when all things were declared "very good" by God (Genesis 1:31), Satan rebelled against God and was cast out of heaven.

"How you have fallen from heaven, O morning star, son of the

Rev. Ezekiel King

dawn! You have been cast down to the earth, you who once laid low the nations!" (Isaiah 14:12).

Jesus said, "I saw Satan fall like lightning from heaven" (Luke 10:18),

"A Star that had fallen from the sky to the earth" (Revelation 9:1).

By all indications, Satan was originally an angel in heaven before becoming a demon. He is the leader of all demons.

Angels exist and so do demons.

Answer 5

The Holy Bible, in Ephesians, warns that Christians do not battle against flesh and blood; but rather, against all manner of evil powers that be in the spiritual and physical world.

29

Rev. Ezekiel King

*12 For our struggle is not
against flesh and blood, but against
the rulers, against the authorities,
against the powers of this dark world
and against the spiritual forces of evil
in the heavenly realms.*

*(Ephesians 6:12   The New
International Version... NIV)*

The old terms used in older Bible versions are 'principalities and powers', 'rulers of the darkness of this world', and the 'spiritual wickedness in high places'. These are demons in action, fully established, but perfectly hidden among humans.

Rev. Ezekiel King

3. ARE DEMONS THE SAME AS EVIL SPIRITS?

Now here is another question that is so confusing to a lot of Christians – are demons the same as evil spirits? I will now answer this question in a wholesome manner.

In nature, everything, living and nonliving, is divided into two main levels of existence…

1. The physical
2. The spiritual

Human beings, who are flesh and blood, are mortals and to the physical aspect of nature do they belong. Our world is a physical one, and it comprises all that we can see, hear or touch, both living and nonliving, both on earth here and outside it (the universe). Living things on the physical level are subdivided into two main groups – plants (trees, flowers, grass, etc.) and animals (man, birds, fishes, cattle, etc.), and of all these, humans are the most superior. This is the physical world as we know it.

The second aspect of existence in nature is far more superior than the physical. Hence, it has been referred to as the 'super'- 'natural' – written as **supernatural** – or the spiritual (spirit world). Humans cannot see hear or sense anything in the spiritual in any way and yet it is there; contains living and nonliving things just like our world.

The Bible gives us to understand that the physical world and all that is in it has its origin in the supernatural world, which existed at the beginning of time. In the Bible book of Genesis, we learn about God's work of creation, how he created the physical world and all living things in it. The Bible goes on to inform us that God is spirit, and those who wish to worship Him must do so in spirit and not physically.

> *24 God is Spirit, and those*
> *who worship Him must worship in*
> *spirit and truth."*
> **John 4:24 New King James*
> *Version (NKJV)*

Christians, do you now understand one reason why God so hates idol worship even if his name is placed on that idol? He is right there and you worship something else as god?

Rev. Ezekiel King

Like the physical, the spiritual world is also subdivided into levels. God, the Most High and supreme ruler of all realms, is the most superior being in existence and his son Jesus Christ is right by his side. The holy creatures of Heaven, angels, etc., are on the second level beneath the supreme God. They worship and serve him. On the third level below the holy creatures of heaven are fallen angels (demons). On the fourth and last level of the spirit world are the immortal souls/spirits of dead people (the ghosts).

All entries just mentioned above are supernatural beings with varied abilities and power. Another term for them is "spirit" beings. Of the four groups above the one that is automatically and utterly evil are the fallen angels, the demons. Hence, another name for demons are evil spirits.

Answer 2

Under certain unusual circumstances, the spirit of a dead person can get trapped in the world of the living (the physical world) and by way of its supernatural abilities, haunt people or even do them harm directly.

33

This sort of cases, though very rare, are quite real and the ghosts are often referred to as evil spirits.

Also see chapter 45: **Are Ghosts and Demons the Same?**

Rev. Ezekiel King

4. CAN DEMONS POSSESS PEOPLE?

Since ancient times, demons have been known to possess (or demonize) living people and this always results in the victim taking on a completely different personality and sometimes, abilities too. For example, their character changes, the tone of their voice becomes different and they may speak in different languages (mostly old languages), they may display remarkable memories and an ability to predict the future, they may even become incredibly strong.

In this situation, some people have been known to remember past lives, recounting events they have no right to remember. You hear the story of a little girl who remembers being a kind 700 years ago, recounting accurately, historic events that even the best historians were not able to capture in their records. You hear of a violently mad person overcoming all those trying to restrain him or breaking free of his restraining iron chains. You see or hear of mad people who can predict the future, reveal the darkest secrets of people's lives and even speak in too many different languages. People see these things and wonder in amazement and shock, but do not know that they are looking at someone possessed by demons.

35

Let's take a look at a story in the Bible where a possessed man encounters Jesus Christ. Let's see what happened.

26 Then they sailed to the country of the [a]Gadarenes, which is opposite Galilee. 27 And when He stepped out on the land, there met Him a certain man from the city who had demons [b]for a long time. And he wore no clothes, nor did he live in a house but in the tombs. 28 When he saw Jesus, he cried out, fell down before Him, and with a loud voice said, "What have I to do with You, Jesus, Son of the Most High God? I beg You, do not torment me!" 29 For He had commanded the unclean spirit to come out of the man. For it had often seized him, and he was kept under guard, bound with chains and shackles; and he broke the bonds and

Rev. Ezekiel King

was driven by the demon into the wilderness.

30 Jesus asked him, saying, "What is your name?"

And he said, "Legion," because many demons had entered him. 31 And they begged Him that He would not command them to go out into the abyss.

32 Now a herd of many swine was feeding there on the mountain. So they begged Him that He would permit them to enter them. And He permitted them. 33 Then the demons went out of the man and entered the swine, and the herd ran violently down the steep place into the lake and drowned.

*Luke 8:26-33 New King James Version (NKJV)

The story above has several lessons to teach us. For one thing, more than one demon can possess a person, and for another, demons recognize the authority of God where ever they meet it. Below is an outline of these facts....

1. **Multiple demons may possess one person**: Many demons can possess a person at the same time. In the case above, the number of demons in the possessed man was so much that they needed an entire herd of swine to shift into.

2. **Demons recognize authority**: In the story above, no one brought the mad (possessed) man to Jesus Christ, but the demons in him surrendered once they set eyes on Jesus. In other words, demons recognize God's authority wherever they meet it. This is exactly what happens when demons encounter powerful men of God, the surrender is instant.

3. **Possessed people can be incredibly strong**: The demons in possessed people can make them incredibly strong, such that they break free from chains.

Rev. Ezekiel King

4. **Possessed people love to live in vile places**: In the case above, the possessed man loved to live in the tombs, a place where the dead are buried and so rejected by the living. Places with a history of murder, death or evil are also favored by possessed people.

5. **Possessed people can often see and reveal the secrets of others**: In the case above do you see how the possessed man reveals that Jesus is the son of God? He does so openly and loudly.

6. **Demons are terrified of** hell: Of note above is the plea of the demons in the possessed man asking not to be driven off into the 'abyss'. The term *abyss* means bottomless pit. This is a term associated with hell.

Drugs, such as cocaine, heroin, and math, when taken to addictive levels, in severe cases, have been known to influence demonic possessions.

Rev. Ezekiel King

How Demonic Possession Works

Man is trichotomous in existence, he is flesh, soul, and spirit. The soul and spirit dwelling inside him makes him whole; a living person. Take away the spirit and mortal man is unconscious as in dreams. Take away the soul and mortal man is dead.

When a demon possesses a person, it takes over ownership of the person's body, turning it into a comfortable home on a spiritual scale, hence no medical test can detect its presence or link it to any medical condition it causes (here is the origin of many sudden and mysterious diseases, mental conditions included).

A demon can possess a person for years without anyone realizing it. In severe cases, however, it can suppress the victim's spirit and take full control of the body.

In cases where there is more than one demon possessing a person, there is usually a conflict of sorts which results in very complicated disorders such as violent insanity.

Rev. Ezekiel King

How many Demon can possess one person at the same time?

The human body is considered the perfect vessel (host or home) by demons and several have been known to crowd into one single body at the same time. When they are too many, they are often referred to as legions or armies.

In the New Testament of the Bible, we are told that: Mary Magdalene was a woman from whom seven demons had been driven out (Luke 8 1-3).

Multiple demons can be in one person.

Also in the book of Luke, we have Jesus Christ confronting a possessed man with many demons in him.

41

> *30 Jesus asked him, saying, "What is your name?"*
>
> *And he said, "Legion," because many demons had entered him. 31 And they begged Him that He would not command them to go out into the abyss.*
>
> *32 Now a herd of many swine was feeding there on the mountain. So they begged Him that He would permit them to enter them. And He permitted them. 33 Then the demons went out of the man and entered the swine, and the herd ran violently down the steep place into the lake and drowned.*
>
> **Luke 8:30-33 New King James Version (NKJV)*

In the above extract, note how the demons refer to themselves as "***Legion***" and gives the reason for this as "***we are many***". On being driven out of the man, the demons of the legion are so many that they possessed an entire herd of pigs who then rush away into the sea where they drowned.

Also in the Bible is the story of Jesus healing a mute man by driving out a demon in him. But the Lord goes on to warn that such a demon, now made homeless, wanders in a place that is like a wasteland. And after a while, when it does not find a new home, it returns to its old home. When it finds that home refurbished, it goes and brings seven more demons and they will all dwell inside the person together, making all the person's troubles many times worse than it originally was (Matthew 12:43-45).

From these narrations, it is perfectly clear that any number of demons can pack themselves into a possessed person. In the worst cases, they can be an entire army of them in one person!

Illnesses Caused by Demonic Possession

Madness, blindness, deafness, dumbness, paralysis, weird body odor, Jesus cured a lot of these illnesses just by driving out the demons in the victims. Some of the most complicated illness mankind suffers today are actually caused by demons/demonic possessions. Driving out the

43

demons from those people lead to instant healing and this is your definition of a modern-day miracle which many men of God perform constantly.

A lot of other illnesses are actually biological in origin and a simple adjustment in lifestyle or some medications can fix things. In certain conditions, so can faith in God. Learn to differentiate between these types of illnesses and treat them accordingly. In all things, remember that man is imperfect in nature and that imperfection is like a high barrier between him and his God and so faith healing does not always work.

One of the most common illnesses caused by demonic possession is insanity.

Rev. Ezekiel King

5. CAN DEMONS POSSESS THE DEAD?

Demons are very powerful supernatural beings that can do a lot of things, but giving new life to the dead is not one of them.

Centuries ago, during the days of the Inquisition, the Catholic Church investigated deeply, the strange rumor that demons could sleep with and impregnate women. One of the theories put forth at the time was that demons took possession of dead bodies, causing them to rise and have sexual intercourse with women. Two of the men that were behind this theory were none other than St. Augustine (5th Century AD) and King James of England and Scotland (1567 – 1627), author of the King James Version of the Holy Bible. Both men gave their input in the form of published works that spanned over 800 years.

St. Augustine stated, "There is also a very general rumor. Many have verified it by their own experience and trustworthy persons

45

have corroborated the experience

others told, that sylvans and fauns,

commonly called incubi, have often

made wicked assaults upon women."

****

King James also shared this

view and in his thesis titled

Dæmonologie, he disproves the

possibility of angelic beings ever

being able to reproduce. He offered,

instead, the suggestion that a demon

could only impregnate a woman in

two ways: the first was to steal the

seed (sperm or semen) out of a dead

man and then transfer it into a

woman. The problem with this theory

is that if a demon or any

supernatural being for that matter

could extract the sperm of a dead

man quickly enough after death, the

transportation of the warm, delicate

Rev. Ezekiel King

> *substance to a female host could*
> *never be instant, resulting in it's*
> *going cold and useless. King James*
> *presented another theory here....*
> *(TOTAL DELIVERANCE*
> *FROM SPIRIT HUSBAND AND*
> *SPIRIT WIFE by Rev. Ezekiel King)*

At the time, this theory caused a lot of fear throughout Christendom and, in many parts, dead bodies were burnt rather than buried. Where dead bodies were buried, stakes were driven through their hearts to ensure they never rose again. Since that early time till today, the idea of demons taking possession of dead bodies has not quite died down and such beings are often called Vampires.

As recently as 2018, a mass grave was unearthed in Italy by some American archeologists from the University of Arizona. The remains of several bodies which had been buried in a vampire-like manner (with stakes driven through their hearts) were discovered there and the most spectacular of them all was that of a 10-year-old boy....

47

Discovered at an ancient Roman site in Umbria, Italy, which dates back to the 15th century, was a mass grave that contained the remains of several bodies. Among these bodies was a very strange one, the remains of a 10-year-old boy with a brick stuffed in his mouth and his legs and arms tied. This ancient method of burial was an alternative to driving a stake through the heart of a vampire. The locals quickly named the boy 'The Vampire of Lugnano' and the fact that tests showed that the child died of a rare strain of malaria did not change that.
*(Are Vampires Real? – IKingreads.com)

The part about demons possessing dead bodies and turning them into vampires and the undead who live forever has a lot more to do with Hollywood movies and superstitions than reality.

Rev. Ezekiel King

6. CAN DEMONS POSSESS ANIMALS?

Yes, demons can possess animals and do so more often than you can ever imagine. Even the Holy Bible itself makes this perfectly clear.

> *30 Now a good way off from them there was a herd of many swine feeding. 31 So the demons begged Him, saying, "If You cast us out, permit us to go away into the herd of swine."*
>
> *32 And He said to them, "Go." So when they had come out, they went into the herd of swine. And suddenly the whole herd of swine ran violently down the steep place into the sea, and perished in the water.*
> **Matthew 8:20-32 New King James Version (NKJV)*

Rev. Ezekiel King

When demons possess animals, the animals may go mad, yes, but in most cases, the demons do such things for very specific purposes and so the animals take on their personality rather than go mad. For example, in the Bible book of Genesis, the devil, the chief of all demons, took on the form of a serpent for the specific purpose of deceiving Eve, the mother of humanity. One of the reasons why that evil trick worked was that the serpent was one of the many nice animals Eve had been seeing in her many walks through the garden of Eden. It is to be noted that at that early time the serpent had legs and was no eater of dust, hence my reference to it as a "nice animal"

> *3 Now the serpent was*
> *cleverer than any other beast of the*
> *field that the Lord God had made. He*
> *said to the woman, "Did God actually*
> *say, 'You[a] shall not eat of any tree*
> *in the garden'?" 2 And the woman*
> *said to the serpent, "We may eat of*
> *the fruit of the trees in the garden, 3*
> *but God said, 'You shall not eat of*
> *the fruit of the tree that is in the*

51

midst of the garden, neither shall you touch it, lest you die.'" 4 But the serpent said to the woman, "You will not surely die. 5 For God knows that when you eat of it your eyes will be opened, and you will be like God, knowing good and evil." 6 So when the woman saw that the tree was good for food, and that it was a delight to the eyes, and that the tree was to be desired to make one wise, [b] she took of its fruit and ate, and she also gave some to her husband who was with her, and he ate. 7 Then the eyes of both were opened, and they knew that they were naked. And they sewed fig leaves together and made themselves loincloths.

8 And they heard the sound of the Lord God walking in the garden in the cool[c] of the day, and the man and his wife hid themselves from the presence of the Lord God among the trees of the garden. 9 But the Lord

God called to the man and said to him, "Where are you?" [d] 10 And he said, "I heard the sound of you in the garden, and I was afraid, because I was naked, and I hid myself." 11 He said, "Who told you that you were naked? Have you eaten of the tree of which I commanded you not to eat?" 12 The man said, "The woman whom you gave to be with me, she gave me fruit of the tree, and I ate." 13 Then the Lord God said to the woman, "What is this that you have done?" The woman said, "The serpent deceived me, and I ate."

14 The Lord God said to the serpent, "Because you have done this, cursed are you above all livestock and above all beasts of the field; on your belly you shall go, and dust you shall eat all the days of your life.

15 I will put enmity between you and the woman, and between

53

> *your offspring[e] and her offspring;*
> *he shall bruise your head, and you*
> *shall bruise his heel."*
>> *(Genesis 3:1-15. NKJV of the*
>> *Holy Bible)*

In that way that demons possess people, so also do they possess animals. The animals take on the demon's personality and the demon is in full control of its body. A demon finds it a lot easier to enter the body of an animal than that of a human, who has a powerful mind and spirit to defend itself. However, demons find human bodies much more comfortable and always make it their first target when seeking a place of rest.

Answer 2

Throughout history, people have always created works of art and idols dissipating demons in the form of frightening animals. Some give them the full appearance of animals while others depict them as half human, half animal creatures (the gods of ancient Egypt were portrayed

Rev. Ezekiel King

this way). There are those that even depict these demonic beings as a union of two or more animals in one.

The interesting thing to note here is that while artists often create things out of their imagination, religious zealots, who build idols, often recreate images of what they have seen in dreams, visions or in reality after demons have manifested themselves to them.

And so, to answer the original question. Demons do take on animal form both physically and spiritually.

Rev. Ezekiel King

7. HOW DOES GOD PUNISH THOSE WHO ASSOCIATE WITH DEMONS?

God's punishment for those who associate with demons, whether intentionally or not, is terrible. For all those who associate/communicate with demons, offer them sacrifices, the possessed, or the tormented; as long as any demon enters your body or life due to sin or otherwise, the consequence is the same – rejection by God, eternal condemnation and death. This is so because there is terrible evil in you and how it got in does not really matter.

One good example we can look to here is to be found in the book of Genesis where Satan takes on the form of a serpent (a snake) in the Garden of Eden to deceive Eve, the mother of humanity, so that she ate of the fruit of the forbidden tree. She also gave the fruit to her husband, Adam, and he too ate it. After that sin, when the two heard the voice of God, they ran to hide in shame…

8 And they heard the sound of
the Lord God walking in the garden
in the cool[c] of the day, and the man

Rev. Ezekiel King

and his wife hid themselves from the presence of the Lord God among the trees of the garden. 9 But the Lord God called to the man and said to him, "Where are you?" [d] 10 And he said, "I heard the sound of you in the garden, and I was afraid, because I was naked, and I hid myself." 11 He said, "Who told you that you were naked? Have you eaten of the tree of which I commanded you not to eat?" 12 The man said, "The woman whom you gave to be with me, she gave me fruit of the tree, and I ate." 13 Then the Lord God said to the woman, "What is this that you have done?" The woman said, "The serpent deceived me, and I ate."

14 The Lord God said to the serpent, "Because you have done this, cursed are you above all livestock and above all beasts of the field; on your belly you shall go, and

Rev. Ezekiel King

dust you shall eat all the days of your life.

15 I will put enmity between you and the woman, and between your offspring[e] and her offspring; he shall bruise your head, and you shall bruise his heel."

(Genesis 3:1-15. NKJV of the Holy Bible)

Note that after that hideous sin of deceiving Eve and damaging humanity, the animal was punished directly by God and not the demon. The same fate awaits all humans who associate with demons in any manner or become possessed by them.

The issue here is very deep-lying. Demons are utterly evil and hated by God. They already have a permanent punishment awaiting them (the torment of hell). Their one aim then is to drag as many other creatures as they can into that hell with them in order to spite God who created all things, living and nonliving.

This is a classic case of a jealous, rebellious and unrepentant evil son destroying everything his father built

Rev. Ezekiel King

and loves. Nonetheless, the father stands firm in his rejection and resolution to punish that child, but only at his own time. Meanwhile, everything that child touches, due to the evil in him, becomes repulsive to the holy father and is automatically condemned. Humans, animals, objects, once touched by demons has evil and sin in them and so are all condemned to death and hell.

And this was the huge problem God faced in the times of long ago before Christ was born. Even in those ancient times, man was an avid sinner and a whole lot of sacrifices and rituals were required to cleanse him of that sin and free him of the associating evil. Too many people, for one reason or the other, could not go through with such expansive and extensive rites each and every single time they sinned. Consequently, too many souls were landing in hell; entire nations of them.

Humanity was in trouble and God knew it.

To have some understanding of this issue read through the old testament. Of all the nations on earth in those ancient times, which did God chose to be his people? Just one nation… Israel. Now even in this situation, how many times did God reject and abandon Israel due to sin? God warned them severally against it through many prophets, yet the sin went on…

59

> *10 Let no one be found*
> *among you who sacrifices their son*
> *or daughter in the fire, who practices*
> *divination or sorcery, interprets*
> *omens, engages in witchcraft, 11 or*
> *casts spells, or who is a medium or*
> *spiritist or who consults the dead. 12*
> *Anyone who does these things is*
> *detestable to the Lord; because of*
> *these same detestable practices the*
> *Lord your God will drive out those*
> *nations before you. 13 You must be*
> *blameless before the Lord your God.*
> **Deuteronomy 18:10-13 New*
> *International Version (NIV)*

All the sins mentioned above are sins inspired by demons and the rewards of demonic possession. Moses was the first prophet to caution the people of Israel about this issue. Isaiah, Hosea, Elijah and other prophets who followed warned the people of Israel against such sins.

Rev. Ezekiel King

Hear, O heavens, and give ear, O earth!

For the Lord has spoken:
"I have nourished and brought up children,
And they have rebelled against Me;
3 The ox knows its owner
And the donkey its master's [a]crib;
But Israel does not know,
My people do not consider."
*Isaiah 1: 2-3 New King James Version (NKJV)

****

When you [g]spread out your hands,
I will hide My eyes from you;
Even though you make many prayers,
I will not hear.

61

Your hands are full of [h]blood.
*Isaiah 1: 15 New King James Version (NKJV)

****

6 My people are destroyed for lack of knowledge: because thou hast rejected knowledge, I will also reject thee, that thou shalt be no priest to me: seeing thou hast forgotten the law of thy God, I will also forget thy children.
Hosea 4:6 King James Version (KJV-)

****

18 "Come now, let us settle the matter,"

Rev. Ezekiel King

says the Lord.

"Though your sins are like scarlet,

they shall be as white as snow;

though they are red as crimson,

they shall be like wool.

19 If you are willing and obedient,

you will eat the good things of the land;

20 but if you resist and rebel,

you will be devoured by the sword."

For the mouth of the Lord has spoken.

Isaiah 1: 18-20 New International Version (NIV)

As you can see, even in those early times, the living God, even in anger, was ready to forgive all who turned back to him. But always the rites of forgiveness of sins and complete cleansing were a huge problem. Man sinned too often and lacked both the funds and will to go through the proper rites of cleansing as many times as he sinned. God had to solve the issue in a general manner time and again…

> *20 "When Aaron has finished making atonement for the Most Holy Place, the tent of meeting and the altar, he shall bring forward the live goat. 21 He is to lay both hands on the head of the live goat and confess over it all the wickedness and rebellion of the Israelites—all their sins—and put them on the goat's head. He shall send the goat away into the wilderness in the care of someone appointed for the task. 22 The goat will carry on itself all their sins to a remote place; and the man shall release it in the wilderness.*
>
> *- Leviticus 16:20-22 New International Version of the Holy Bible (NIV)*

Rev. Ezekiel King

After each rite of cleansing, the people would sin again and be on their way to death with no easy alternative. To solve this problem once and for all, God sent Jesus Christ!

> *16 For God so loved the world that he gave his one and only Son, that whoever believes in him shall not perish but have eternal life.*
> **John 3:16 New International Version (NIV)*

And there you have it, God's final solution to sin. Even today there are people called mediums, those who practice evil divination and those who offer sacrifices to false gods. Don't look too far, some of them are the heads of the churches you attend each Sunday (false prophets and pastors) and multitudes of people follow them straight to hell. Some are even your friends and neighbors.

In today's world, we must be careful of those we associate with and try to learn a thing or two about their lifestyles. Still, this may not save us from being the targets

Rev. Ezekiel King

of demons and we have them in our lives even without relapsing it.

To avoid the ultimate consequence of sin and association with demons, Jesus Christ is your answer. Confess that sin, turn away from it and walk in the light, all in Jesus name and it will be well with you.

Rev. Ezekiel King

8. CAN HUMAN BEINGS SEE DEMONS?

Now, here is a very complicated question for which there is no straight answer.

By all the laws of nature, it is impossible for human beings, mere mortals, to see, hear or sense demons, invincible supernatural beings that they are. However, some supernatural entities have the ability to reveal themselves directly to people, taking clear form and shape before them.

> *15 A spirit glided past my face and the hair on my body stood on end.*
> **Job 4:15 New International Version (NIV)*

Note that not all supernatural or spiritual beings have the ability to reveal themselves to people and even some of those that can choose not to do so. For example, the living God can reveal himself directly to mankind but chooses not to do so because such a high level of pure holiness and power, which he is, is deadly to mankind. No living person can see God and live.

> *18 Then Moses said, "Now show me your glory."*
> *19 And the Lord said, "I will cause all my goodness to pass in front of you, and I will proclaim my name, the Lord, in your presence. I will have mercy on whom I will have mercy, and I will have compassion on whom I will have compassion. 20 But," he said, "you cannot see my face, for no one may see me and live."*
> **Exodus 33:18-21 New International Version (NIV)*

Indeed, no one can see God's face and live. It's a natural fact. However, God is the most superior supernatural being alive. Lesser supernatural beings who

Rev. Ezekiel King

were created by God do not have this extreme effect on humans and demons are one of them.

Some demons truly reveal themselves to people both in reality and in dreams, taking clear form and shape.

Answer 2

In rare cases, in the religious worship of God, some special individuals are blessed with the divine gift of spiritual awareness, which gives them the unusual ability to see, hear and, or, sense demons. This special ability is completely different from normal human vision, hearing or sensory abilities.

Of the three abilities, the most common is that of spiritual vision and it varies in strength from person to person. Some pastors and other such servants of God are blessed with this gift but cannot hear or sense the presence of supernatural beings clearly (such a thing as a demon hiding in the body of a person can escape their notice entirely).

However, there are those who possess all three abilities (prophets) and I am one. Personally, I can see, hear and sense the presence of demons and any other spiritual

Rev. Ezekiel King

beings, both in a conscious state (when wide awake) and in an unconscious state (in a dream or when asleep). I can sense them even when they are inside animals, trees, houses or people. I'm not alone in this ability and it's still growing in strength.

In my experience, demons love to possess three kinds of animals in particular; cats, dogs, and birds. As for people, they prefer to possess women, very beautiful women, a lot more than.

Answer 3

Mediums are humans blessed with the ability to see, hear and sense the presence of supernatural beings. The thing to note about mediums is that, like witches and magicians, it is not God who gave them that amazing 'blessing' or ability, but demons living within them. Hence, their power is only effective with supernatural beings on the demonic level of existence downward – this is the lower levels of existence in the spirit world.

Simply put, mediums can effectively see, hear or sense demons and ghosts only. Still, even here, the ability varies in strength from person to person.

Rev. Ezekiel King

Now, you know why God hates mediums and witches so much.

Answer 4

Humans have direct access to the spirit world in one strange way and there, they often encounter demons of all kinds, seeing, hearing and sensing them clearly even without realizing it.

Ever slept and dreamt about encountering a dead loved one or even getting attacked by a strange person or animal?

Whenever you sleep and dream, one of two things is happening. Either your mind is playing games on you or your spirit has left your body to wander.

In the first case, the mind (also the brain) does things like make a person relive past experiences or events of his or her life. In the second case, where the spirit leaves the body to wander during dreams, that *wandering* is actually done at the lowest level of the spirit world where it often encounters the spirits of both the dead and other living people. So how does it encounter demons?

71

In that way people can take an occasional walk in the forest or a dive in the sea, both of which are home to lesser animals such as deer, fishes, whales, bears, etc., so also can higher supernatural beings stop into the world of lesser ones. Demons are constantly prowling the "dream world" and can take different forms to interact directly with the spirits of living people or even attack them.

Many people take things like this for granted when they wake up, it's just another bad dream that means nothing, but in reality, they have encountered demons.

The thing is, in human form, we may not be able to see or sense supernatural beings in any way, but in spiritual form such as in dreams, we stand a better chance of doing this.

Unfortunately, that ability is very limited because we are not completely spirit and so do not belong in the spiritual world. We are merely visitors there and that visit is only possible because man is trichotomous in existence; he is flesh, soul, and spirit. The soul is the one connection between the flesh and the spirit. When a person is alive, the soul is firmly rooted in the body (flesh). The spirit may wander outside the body from time to time when a person is unconscious, but as long as the soul stays rooted in the body it must return and the person awakens.

Rev. Ezekiel King

A person dies only when the soul finally leaves the body. It then becomes one with the spirit and that person becomes wholly spirit. Some call these spirits of the dead ghosts.

Ghost exist at the lowest level of the spirit world. They are the least powerful there and are mostly in a state of rest.

Rev. Ezekiel King

9. ARE HUMANS DEMONS?

No, humans are not demons and can never become demons under any circumstance.

Demons, like angels, are supernatural beings. They are far more superior in nature to humans, despite losing most of their angelic powers in the day they sinned and were cast out of heaven. Humans, on the other hand, are mortals who are very limited in ability.

A demon can possess (live inside) a person, but a person cannot possess or dwell inside a demon. When possessed, a person can act, talk and think like a demon, but afterwards, when that demon has been driven out of that person's body, the victim often has no recollection of his or her actions. Medical science, under psychiatry/psychology, has a very broad theory in place to explain away this strange phenomenon in humans and it ranges from mental blackouts to psych episodes.

Rev. Ezekiel King

10. WHAT CAN DEMONS DO?

In the day demons sinned against God and were cast out of heaven, they were completely stripped of their holiness, which carries a lot of power and great authority. All they have now are their powers as supernatural beings of high order, but even so, that power is still very considerable by any human standard.

Demons can do quite a lot of things, most of which are amazing and so baffling to ignorant humans who possess very limited abilities as mortals. However, due to their evil nature, nothing done by a demon is good. Some demons might deceive people into thinking they are good in nature; doers of good, but there is always a hidden price to be paid for that good deed and it's usually terrible - this is basically the root of demonic covenants and curses (we will deal with this much later). THERE IS NO SUCH THING AS A GOOD DEMON.

Below is a list of some of the things demons can do and constantly do...

1. Demons can possess people

Rev. Ezekiel King

2. Demons can make people think and do exactly what they want.

3. Demons confuse the truth by making up demonic half-truths and lies (1 John 4:4). (Family or relationship conflicts, false churches, fake religions, etc. all these exist because of demonic confusion.)

4. Demons often parade themselves as good spirits or gods.

5. Some demons can take different forms and shapes; can even appear to be people.

6. Demons can move objects around without being seen.

7. Demons can induce all manner of complicated sickness in people, including deafness, blindness, madness, etc.

8. Some demons can induce superhuman strength in people and even give them other abilities like with witches, wizards, and mediums.

9. Demons can cause mysterious damages to objects, such as electronic and electrical gadgets, in a home.

The list is endless! In truth, demons can do almost anything from raping and impregnating women directly to impersonating, deceiving and confusing people on a grand scale, causing great trouble even in families and other relationships. They have even been known to take possession of people for the purpose of leading them to commit suicide, murder, rape, and a lot of other atrocities.

Some demons that depict themselves as "gods" to be worshiped have been known to solve problems for people, heal sickness and even bring about wealth. But unknown to the thankful people, receiving these good things, such "blessing", effectively places them in a demonic covenant that binds them to that demon forever in life and death. When this sort of covenant is broken in any manner, a terrible curse or consequence follows; death, disaster, destruction, etc.

Of note is that there is no such thing as equality among demons. Their abilities depend on their rank, strength, and power. All these facts are explained in different chapters of this book.

11. WHAT ARE THE LIMITATION OF DEMONS?

Perhaps another way to put this question is, what can't demons do? There are few things that demons cannot do, powerful supernatural beings that they are, but they do have their limitations and therein lies their weakness.

The two most important things demons cannot do, are not permitted to do, and can never do even if they tried hard, thanks to God, are what keeps human beings and their world from being overrun by these invincible evil creatures.

A demon can never ever do the following...

1. Invade a person's life, home or body without invitation.
2. Enter a truly Holy Place.

Fear, lust, anger, hate, etc., any manner of sin or doubt in God is more than enough to open the door to these demons. This is the invitation.

A holy place is a place where the Spirit of God resides in a manner that is not harmful to humans or anything good, but deadly to all evil. There are only a few truly "holy places" left on earth, full of sin as it is, and all of them are religious places of worship, mostly churches. However, so many churches today are not holy places, hence a possessed person can keep attending church for years and feel nothing at all. In many truly "holy" churches, for the safety of the people, who can be sinful by nature, the holy place is restricted to the raised area of the altar where only the men of God are allowed to go, but the grace and power of God cover the entire church.

A holy place is a place of refuge for all victims of demonic attacks. No demon can follow you there, not even when it is living right inside the person (possessed people) - it must leave even if temporarily.

Items blessed and taken from a holy place, such as water or oil, can be used in cleansing and fortifying the body, a house or a specific area against the attacks of demons. Sprinkling or rubbing the liquid all over the affected place or area is enough and that place or area will remain holy and inaccessible to demons until a sin is committed there, whether knowingly or unknowingly.

Answer 2

79

Rev. Ezekiel King

Man may not be as powerful as demons, but in God, he has authority over all demons. Demons have no real power over people except that which people give them. One of the first people to discover this fact was the incredibly wise King Solomon and he exploited it to the full.

In his little known book, ***The Testament of Solomon,*** King Solomon details how he enslaved some of the most powerful demons in the world of darkness to help build his temple.

In those times of long ago, man needed to perform certain rites to subdue demons, but today, things have changed for Christians. By the simple words of your mouth in the name of Jesus, you can set a boundary in your life and no demon will cross it.

Rev. Ezekiel King

12. HOW MANY DEMONS ARE THERE IN EXISTENCE?

There is no precise answer to this question. Nowhere in the Bible is this question asked or answered in any clear manner. However, the Bible does give us some hint to things when certain verses are lined up together, throw in some divine knowledge and things get very interesting.

A long time ago, after the creation of the angels of heaven, came the creation of the earth and all that is in it. At about the period known to man as that sixth day of creation, when God declared the everything was "very good" and pleasing to His eyes (Genesis 1:31), the highest ranking angel in heaven rebelled against God and was cast out of heaven. (Very detailed revelations of the events of creation are given in my book ***Creation vs Evolution***)

The name of that angel, the highest ranking angel of the time, was Lucifer, prince of the morning.

"How you have fallen from heaven, O morning star, son of the

81

dawn! You have been cast down to the earth, you who once laid low the nations!" (Isaiah 14:12).

Jesus said, "I saw Satan fall like lightning from heaven" (Luke 10:18)

"A star that had fallen from the sky to the earth" (Revelation 9:1).

The Holy Bible goes on to tell us that a third of the "innumerable company of angels" chose to rebel with Satan (Hebrews 12:22).

Take note now of the word used in the Bible verse above to describe the number of angels in heaven at the time of Satan's rebellion… **innumerable**. The word **innumerable** is used when something is so great in number that a specific figure cannot be put to them. Another word that can be used here is countless.

In the book of the Revelations, the Apostle John reaffirmed this incredible fact with a vision of great wonder in heaven…

Rev. Ezekiel King

"...an enormous red dragon...His tail swept a third of the stars out of the sky and flung them to the earth...the great dragon was hurled down—that ancient serpent called the devil, or Satan, who leads the whole world astray. He was hurled to the earth, and his angels with him" (Revelation 12:3–9).

Now, let's line the facts up.

The Bible refers to Satan severally as a star which was cast out of heaven and fell down to the earth. In the Book of Revelation, it is made clear that a third of the stars were cast out with Satan. There is even another depiction of an evil dragon plucking out a third of the stars from the sky and casting them down to the earth.

The facts are so clear that they are hard to misunderstand. The stars in Revelations refer to the fallen angels who were with Satan. They are one-third of the total heavenly host, which are numberless.

83

We now know two things. Firstly, there is a great number of demons with Satan; a third of the numberless host of heaven.

Secondly, Satan may have one-third of the armies of heaven on his side, but God still has two thirds on his side, and for followers of Jesus Christ, God's angels are on our side as well.

Rev. Ezekiel King

13. WHO IS THE LEADER OF DEMONS?

Satan, also known as the devil, is the leader of all demons. He is the most powerful of them all as well. At one time, he was the highest ranking angel in heaven and was called Lucifer, Prince of the Morning. But after he rebelled and was cast out of heaven, he lost all holiness and authority and became known as Satan, prince of darkness.

In the **Testament of Solomon**, where King Solomon describes how, with the help of Archangel Michael, he enslaved the most powerful demons on earth to build his temple, he tells us about a very powerful demon who called himself **Beelzebul.**

The demon Beelzebul revealed to Solomon that he was formerly the highest ranking angel in Heaven!

Clearly, the demon Beelzebul is none other than the devil himself. The interesting thing here is that the name Beelzebul is the Greek version of the name Beelzebub, who was a pagan god worshipped by the ancient Philistines who built a great temple to his name in the Philistine city of Ekron during the era of the Old Testament. A shortened form of that name Beelzebub is Baal (Beel-zebub). This is

85

the same Baal, whose worship was introduced into Israel in the time of Elijah, who served as a prophet before God in the day Ahab was King of Israel and Jezebel was his queen.

The Great Deceiver

Of all the demons, the one that is powerful enough to and fondest of impersonating God is Satan. He is the one that deceives whole nations by portraying himself as God and creator of all things.

Over the ages, people of different lands and clime have worshipped Satan as one god or the other. He is the pagan god with many names, the god of idols and the eater of human blood sacrifices. This was his way in the past, but with the establishment of the Christian church and religion by Jesus Christ, Satan's operations evolved.

Today, Satan is the demon behind the establishment of the Church of Satan, an international organization with multitudes of followers around the world. The religion of Satanism and cultism have been just as popular.

Rev. Ezekiel King

14. IS THE WORLD OF DEMONS A CHAOTIC PLACE?

Demons may be well known for causing chaos and confusion on earth among humans, but there is no such thing in their own world.

The Bible gives us to understand that demons are well organized under Satan in hierarchical levels (ranks) known as rulers, authorities (principalities), and powers. Combined, they are the spiritual forces of evil...

> *10 Finally, be strong in the Lord and in his mighty power. 11 Put on the full armor of God, so that you can take your stand against the devil's schemes. 12 For our struggle is not against flesh and blood, but against the rulers, against the authorities, against the powers of this dark world and against the spiritual forces of evil in the heavenly realms.*

87

Rev. Ezekiel King

Ephesians 6:10-12 New
International Version (NIV)

Every demon has its specific task and position in the world of darkness. Satan is the undisputed leader and ruler of that evil world.

Rev. Ezekiel King

15. HOW MANY TYPES OF DEMONS ARE THERE?

In the study of demonology, one of the most common ways in which types of demons are classified is by domain. When demons are classified this way, in types by their domain, the demons get credited to a specific activity (such as mortal sin, dubious behavior or vile knowledge; all of which people are prone to) or inducing sicknesses, misfortunes, or addictions. Every demon within a domain has its own abilities and tasks according to its power (authority), and these demons (each one) interact with human beings in very unique ways.

Throughout the ages, people have always attempted to classify the different types of demons in various ways with respect to their domains and below are three lists that give you an idea of what the subject is about.

Here are the different types of demons grouped according to their domains with respect to the deadliest sins of humanity.

Deadly Sin 1: **Pride**

Demon Type – **Lucifer** ✓

Deadly Sin 2: Envy
Demon Type: Beelzebub ✓

Deadly Sin 3: **Greed**
Demon Type: **Mammon** ✓

Deadly Sin 4: **Wrath**
Demon Type: **Satan** ✓

Deadly Sin 5: **Sloth**
Demon Type: **Abaddon** ✓

Deadly Sin 6: **Lust**
Demon Type: **Asmodeus** ✓

Deadly Sin 7: **Gluttony**
Demon Type: **Belphegor** ✓

Answer 2

Rev. Ezekiel King

Demon types can also be drawn up according to how they work and the problems they cause. For example, some demons like Baal depict themselves as gods to be worshipped while others lead people into witchcraft, assault people in all kinds of ways and even rape and impregnate women directly.

The list below is a lot more realistic when compared to the different types of demons in existence today. It is very similar to that put forth by Alphonso de Spina, in the year 1467, but not quite.

- **Demons of fate** –Demons of death, destruction, nightmares, and sickness.
- **Incubus and Succubus demons**: These are sex demons that exploit lust and have sex with humans (for more information on this subject, see my book ***Spiritual Husband and Spiritual Wife: Incubus and*** Succubus)
- **Legions**: Wandering demons. They can be in groups or armies when possessing someone.
- **Familiar Demons** – These are personal demons or spirits that guide witches, wizard,

91

mediums, magicians and other humans who practice such evils

- **Mischievous demons:** Trouble and problem causing demons that exploit all manner of weakness in people, including the seven deadly sins.

- **Demi-gods**: Also called demigods, these are
  - demons that lure people into worshiping them through false religions, principles, and beliefs.

Answer 3

Based on other theological studies, below is yet another list of demons and devils. Packed into this list are the actual identities of some of the most dangerous demons one can ever encounter. On close observation, you will find similarities between this list and the other two above.

1. False Gods – Beelzebub, Baal
2. Vengeful Spirits – Asmodeus
3. Iniquitous Spirits – Belial
4. Lying Spirits – Pytho

Rev. Ezekiel King

5. Deluding Spirits – Balban

6. Creators of tempests – The Powers that be in the Air

7. Furies – Powers of Evil, War, and Discord

8. Accusers and Legions

9. Tempters – Mammon

Rev. Ezekiel King

16. HOW DOES ONE BECOME POSSESSED BY A DEMON?

There are so many different ways one can become possessed or even invite demons into one's life, but the quickest of them all is to become a sinner. When you become a sinner, depending on your age, sex and mentality, one or more demons can take possession of your body as was the case of Mary Magdalene, who had seven demons in her, and many theologians have argued, was most likely a prostitute before meeting and following Jesus.

> *8Soon afterwards he went on through cities and villages, proclaiming and bringing the good news of the kingdom of God. The twelve were with him, 2as well as some women who had been cured of evil spirits and infirmities: Mary, called Magdalene, from whom seven demons had gone out, 3and Joanna, the wife of Herod's steward Chuza,*

Rev. Ezekiel King

> **and Susanna, and many others, who**
> **provided for them* out of their**
> **resources.**
>
> **(Luke 8 1-3 NKJV)**

Additionally, fooling around and talking carelessly with certain objects such an Ouija board, a spirit board or even mirrors might not be as simple or ordinary as it appears. In fact, it is dangerous and stupid, as this can summon a demon or demons and you will never be able to control them.

Talking anyhow to demonic entities (or even having them in mind) in the dead of night can also result in this. It's a lot like praying to the wrong god. They will answer and you will be controlled. You will not have power over anything they decide to do with you or to make you do.

Joining an evil occult is another way to get possessed by demons.

95

17. CAN HUMANS BECOME DEMONS?

Human beings cannot become demons under any circumstance. Humans and demons are very different entities with different abilities and makeup. Demons are entirely spiritual (or supernatural) beings while humans, on the other hand, are mortals.

Some might put forth the argument that humans become spirits after death and so could also become demons. This is not even possible at all.

Supernatural (or spiritual) beings, collectively, are not equal in power and have different levels of existence. God, the creator of all things, is the most powerful supernatural being and he exists at the highest level of the spiritual world with his only son right beside him. Angels come next, then demons and finally comes the spirit souls of humans.

Answer 2

Rev. Ezekiel King

It has also been argued that when a person lives a very evil life; a life of total wickedness in which he or she always does the vilest of things, such as killing and torturing animals and humans, associating with evil spirits/demons and making evil sacrifices, etc., that person, at death, becomes a demon and is often worshiped. This assumption is very wrong.

No matter how deeply a person allows his or herself to sink into evil, there is no turning into a demon after death. What usually happens is that at some point, such an evil person becomes possessed by one or more demons and after the person's death, such a demon or demons attempt to fool people by impersonating that person's spirit, giving the impression that the evil person has become a powerful spiritual entity in full transition. A lot of cults have started this way, one of the most famous of which is the cult of Dracula.

Count Dracula was originally a wealthy nobleman who lived in Hungary, Eastern Europe, centuries ago. He built a great reputation for himself as a vampire by torturing and murdering people and drinking their blood.

The movies, novels, and folklore are full of tales of an undying Dracula and the cults centered around him are just as many.

97

Another example is Buddhism. Apart from Christianity and Islam, Buddhism is the largest religion on earth and is practiced by most people in eastern Asia. About 2,000 years ago (400 BC), the founder of Buddhism was a very wealthy prince by the name of Siddhartha Gautama with lands in Nepal, north-east India. He renounced his luxurious lifestyle for one of spirituality, gathered disciples and followers, and assumed the title of Buddha, which means "The Enlightened One". He lived to about 80 years of age, suffered from diarrhea, for most of that time and finally died after eating of pork served by a blacksmith.

Today, between China, Japan, India, Korea and all the other lesser island nations in the region, there are over a billion worshipers of Buddha and thousands of temples.

Rev. Ezekiel King

18. WHAT IS EXORCISM?

Exorcism is a word borrowed from ancient Greek and means, "binding by oath" or "to bind by oath". It is the spiritual or religious practice of casting out demons from an area, place or person believed to be possessed, either in the name of a superior being or by oath. This is normally done to relieve certain symptoms of sicknesses, mental illness or unusual behavior and, or sinister occurrences.

Exorcism has its origins in the early Christian Church, but contrary to many beliefs that it is practiced only in Christianity, it is part of the belief system of quite a number of cultures and religions.

The act of exorcism, which has been in use by the Christian Church (the Catholic Church in particular) for more than 1,100 years, entails performing an elaborate rite that ends with commanding the demon or demons to depart the possessed in the name of Jesus Christ. An exorcism is an elaborate rite that is performed by an exorcist, a special kind of priest. Therefore, it is not surprising that the primary tools normally used are closely associated with Cartelism – a crucifix, a Bible, and holy water. Prayers in the original Latin words are usually used.

99

A Priest exorcizing a possessed woman.

The belief in the evil activities of demons among humans, causing sicknesses, sufferings and misfortune's, was very strong in ancient times and so exorcism was constantly requested and performed by professional exorcists trained by the Catholic Church. However, all that began to decline by the 18th century and by the mid-20th century, there was no such thing as a professional exorcist anymore.

However, with the advent of so many powerful demon-based movies like ***The Exorcist*** and the excessive publicity given to the evil activities of demons by so many churches, exorcism has now become refined and more of a profit based business than anything else. The elaborate rites

Rev. Ezekiel King

are gone and it's all about driving out demons by all and any means possible. Today, you will find pastors, religious leaders and other fraudulent characters raking in huge financial profits off the troubles of innocent believers by attempting to cure illnesses and other disorders through casting out demons even where nothing exists but a normal health issue that requires urgent medical attention.

Many years ago, I stumbled across a church where people take insane relatives and loved ones for healing. The church ran a private healing school where these insane people are held in chains and made to undergo daily exorcism and torture on route to healing. The most common torture methods utilized here was to flog these unfortunate victims with horsewhips and wires to within an inch of their lives. The cries of these tormented souls during this period of torture was blood-chilling.

The idea behind this process, according to the church officials, was that, with time, demons would leave the body of a physically tormented person. In other words, where all the binding and casting out of the demons do not work, brute force and violence do!

The idea behind this process, according to the church officials, was that, with time, demons would leave the body of a physically tormented person. In other words,

101

where all the binding and casting out of the demons do not work, brute force and violence do!

Classic Prayers in Exorcism

Below are three classic prayers in the old Catholic rite of exorcism or casting out demons and evil spirits.

1. We drive you away from us, whoever you may be, demons or unclean spirits, all infernal invaders, all satanic powers, all wicked legions, assemblies, and sects...

2. Thus, cursed dragon, and you, diabolical legions, we adjure you by the living God, by the true God, by the one most holy God, by the God "who so loved the world that He gave up His only begotten Son, that every soul believing in Him might not perish but have life everlasting;"

3. Leave this place thou demon. [St. John. 3:16] Stop deceiving human creatures and pouring out

Rev. Ezekiel King

to them the poison of eternal damnation; stop harming the Church and hindering her liberty.

Depending on the religious denomination, the circumstance, and the person performing the exorcism, these prayers may differ in wording but the basics are the same. The invading demon is always ordered to leave.

Answer 2

In Christianity, modern exorcism is a bit different from ancient exorcism, which is basically an elaborate rite. For one thing, the compulsory use of prayers solely in the Latin language is no more as are the uses of the crucifix and candle. Christians have done away with these things as they have come to realize that the main power to cast out those demons lies in the name of Jesus Christ and nowhere else.

Today, a more direct approach is taken in casting out demons and the term *exorcism* is rarely ever used to describe it.

Rev. Ezekiel King

Answer 3

As mentioned earlier, exorcism is also practiced in many religions and cultures besides Christianity. However, the way in which things are done is very much different. The casting out of demons from the possessed is not done in the name of Jesus Christ and sometimes, the outgoing demon is usually bound to an oath. And here lies one of the greatest secrets behind the success of false prophets, fake pastors and churches, false gods/pagan gods and cult worshipers, all of which are demonic in origin.

1 Dear friends, do not believe every spirit, but test the spirits to see whether they are from God, because many false prophets have gone out into the world. 2 This is how you can recognize the Spirit of God: Every spirit that acknowledges that Jesus Christ has come in the flesh is from God, 3 but every spirit that does not acknowledge Jesus is not from God.

Rev. Ezekiel King

This is the spirit of the antichrist,
which you have heard is coming and
even now is already in the world. 4
You, dear children, are from God and
have overcome them, because the one
who is in you is greater than the one
who is in the world.

1 John 4:1-4

Too many times we see new churches open one day and get packed with thousands of believers the next week because the prophet/pastor/leader there is performing a thousand miracles a day! But he is also making huge financial profits by mixing worship with all kinds of payment and donation systems! People overlook the money part and focus on the amazing miracles even though it soon becomes very obvious that only select people are getting them, after all, miracles are from God, aren't they? The same scenario plays out with false or pagan gods with priests and worshipers in attendance. The miracles, the blessing, the instant healing, the prophecies, they are there and have been there for generations so the gods are good spirits, aren't they?

105

STOP RIGHT THERE!!!

Demons are not equals. They are arranged in ranks according to authority and power. There are also different types of demons, and they are all classified according to what they do. Bottom line, every demon has its position and task in the demonic realm. The demons that roam the earth causing troubles, sickness, and suffering among humans are mostly lower and mid-level demons. On the other hand, the ones that sit back and play god are high ranking demons like Satan. They are the false gods/pagan gods/demi-gods, the power behind the establishment of many fake churches, temples, and shrines. They are the origin of all the amazing power you see displayed by false prophets, pastors, and priests of today.

When a demon hits a person with sickness, suffering or troubles and the victim is brought before a false god or its servant the false prophets, what happens is exorcism on a demonic scale. The possessing demon, which is definitely a lesser demon, is ordered to leave in the name of the greater demon and once it obeys, what you have is instant healing… a miracle! But unknown to the victim, that miracle has placed you into a covenant with the demon that is binding in life and death. The consequence for breaking such evil covenants is a curse that may result

Rev. Ezekiel King

in sicknesses, disaster, endless misfortune/bad luck or even swift death. Curses like these have been known to be effective for many generations.

Rev. Ezekiel King

19. WHO CAN EXORCISE DEMONS?

In times of long ago, people strongly believed that sicknesses, mental illness, unusual behavior in a person or constant misfortunes in a home, were all caused by the presence of demons and evil spirits and casting out those evil beings was seen as the only solution. The act or ritual of casting out those demons or evil spirits, *exorcism*, could only be performed by a priest in the name of **Jesus Christ**.

Today, medical science has established that most of these sickness and other problems have very legitimate explanations and solutions (cures), and this has led people into making the wrong assumptions that demons never existed in the first place and so could never take possession of people or anything else for that matter. So many people now see "exorcism" as a joke. Some do it for entertainment while others simply do it for financial gain, there are even those who do it out of misplaced devoutness.

There are two dangers here…

1. When the ritual of exorcism is undertaken in a misguided attempt to assist a sick or mentally ill person, where strict medical assistance is

repaired, death or a critical escalation of the problem may result.

2. When the ritual of exorcism is undertaken by someone without the correct spiritual authority or guidance, it could be very dangerous for all involved as the demon or demons being exorcized could become very violent or simply bring more of their kind into play. Since ancient times, demons have been known to attack people who try to exorcise them, including genuine priests.

Just about anyone can attempt to exercise, drive out, or cast out a demon from a possessed person, however, this may be very dangerous where there is a lack of faith, lack of power, lack of knowledge and the presence of any sin at all. The exorcist can become victim number 2 and then things will get worse for everyone. Additionally, if that exorcism is not followed by strict cleaning and a Godly way of life, it could still be very dangerous. Without adequate spiritual care, the victim might then be laid open for a sevenfold infestation of demons (Matthew 12:45).

Rev. Ezekiel King

Answer 2

According to records, there was a time the Catholic Church used to produce professional exorcists – priests specially trained to cast out demons through exorcism. That time is long gone and some of the priests in the Church today don't even recognize the existence of demons.

Furthermore, the rite of exorcism in the old way is not something that is commonly practiced today. For example, the use of Latin prayers and the brandishing of the crucifix are not so common anymore.

Still, the most qualified people to cast out demons remain priests and other divinely anointed men of God. It is their task before God and in his name.

Rev. Ezekiel King

20. WHO CAN CAST OUT DEMONS

For clarification reasons, we have not joined this subject with the previous one which states "Who can exorcise demons?". Exorcism is an elaborate ritual, particular to the Catholic Church and to be done by priests only, while casting out demons directly in the name of Jesus Christ is what many Christians do today.

The one from whom all authority over demons comes unto Christians is Jesus Christ and he first gave it to his disciples and after them, unto all Christians and believers alike.

*Jesus called his twelve
disciples to him and gave them
authority to drive out impure spirits
and to heal every disease and
sickness. (Matthew 10:1)*

*****

Rev. Ezekiel King

Behold, I give unto you power
to tread on serpents and scorpions,
and over all the power of the enemy:
and nothing shall by any means hurt
you.
        - Luke 10:19 King James
Version (KJV)

But there is a catch, and it lies in your mind and the way in which you use the authority. Demons will capitalize on any weakness in you....

13 Some Jews who went
around driving out evil spirits tried to
invoke the name of the Lord Jesus
over those who were demon-
possessed. They would say, "In the
name of the Jesus whom Paul
preaches, I command you to come
out." 14 Seven sons of Sceva, a
Jewish chief priest, were doing this.
15 One day the evil spirit answered
them, "Jesus I know, and Paul I

                                        Rev. Ezekiel King

know about, but who are you?" 16
Then the man who had the evil spirit
jumped on them and overpowered
them all. He gave them such a
beating that they ran out of the house
naked and bleeding.

Acts 19:13-16

As long as you are a Christian/believer, the authority and power to drive out demons are in you. The problem lies in your faith and belief system. Do not leave room for doubt in your mind when going up against any demon for that effectively strips you of all authority and power and the demon will see that.

See also: **"How do you get rid of demons in a home?"**

113

21. DOES EXORCISM ALWAYS WORK AGAINST DEMONS?

Exorcism, the ancient ritual of casting out demons and evil spirits from possessed people, areas or places, does not always work and sometimes, has been known to take too long (an entire year or more). A lot depends on the spiritual abilities (faith or strength) and dedication of the exorcist and the power of the demon being exorcized. In too many cases, the attacker (exorcist) has ended up becoming the attacked.

In the early fifteenth century (the 1400s), the Christian world was shaken by the publication of a German book titled ***Malleus Maleficarum***, written by a Catholic clergyman Heinrich Kramand. That book quickly became famous and was transcribed into English as '**Hammer of Witches**'. This book was one of the first to openly recognize the existence of witches and demons and outline proper ways to deal with them, one of which was exorcism. However, a Franciscan friar of the time named Ludovico Maria Sinistrari had something odd to say about exorcism…

Rev. Ezekiel King

Five ways were recommended by the Malleus Maleficarum to overcome the attacks of the Incubi demon and the very first of them was exorcism. The others were Sacramental Confession, the recital of the Angelic Salutation (or Sign of the Cross), moving the victim to another location, and lastly excommunication of the demonic entity, "which sounds a lot like an exorcism.

Interestingly, a Franciscan friar of the time named Ludovico Maria Sinistrari stated clearly that Incubi demons "do not obey exorcists, have no dread of exorcisms, show no reverence for holy things, at the approach of which they are not in the least overawed"

In other words, the five methods of overcoming the attacks of the Incubus demon as stated by the book The Hammer of Witches (or

115

The Malleus Maleficarum) has been tested and found shockingly ineffective. And so we must now return to our own period and time to find solutions to this problem. However, let's first take a look at some regional variation of the Incubi or Incubus demon.

*Total Deliverance Form Spiritual Husband and Spiritual Wife: Incubus and Succumbs, Incubus Demons, by Rev. Ezekiel King. Buy Book

As I have already stated, exorcism or plain casting out of demons does not always work because a lot depends on the level of authority held by the exorcist and the rank and power of the demon being exorcized.

Answer 2

Rev. Ezekiel King

In Christianity today, the rite of exorcism is more about authoritative prayers, commands, faith and the use of holy items such as holy water, oils and the Holy Bible, in the **name of Jesus Christ**. However, the most important thing for success here is that the act must be done by a true man of God with authority over evil and some measure of "experience", all in the **name of Jesus Christ**.

Why add experience?

Demons that possess people, in particular, have the nasty habit of challenging anyone who attempts to drive them out of that already established home. Apart from becoming very violent, some demons can start up a verbal attack in different languages, both old and new, divulging all kinds of private information about the exorcist and questioning every authority, all in a bid to break the confidence of that exorcist and instill fear and confusion.

Normally, when faced with such demons, the best way to deal with them is with final authority. This is how I do it with a powerful command of a prayer….

Whatever demon you are,
whoever you may be, wherever you
may have come from, in the name of

117

Rev. Ezekiel King

Jesus Christ, who through death
conquered the world and all evil,
LEAVE THIS PLACE NOW!!!

No demon shall stand before the final authority that is in the name of Jesus Christ. It shall be well with all of you tormented by demons.

Amen!

Rev. Ezekiel King

22. ARE BIRTHMARKS SIGNS OF DEMONIC POSSESSION?

Birthmarks are blemishes on the skin of individuals that were in place during the time of their birth or appear soon afterwards.

> *A birthmark is a congenital, benign irregularity on the skin, which is present at birth or appears shortly after birth, usually in the first month. They can occur anywhere on the skin. Birthmarks are caused by the overgrowth of blood vessels, melanocytes, smooth muscle, fat, fibroblasts, or keratinocytes.*
> *- Wikipedia*

Some birthmarks are minor while other a large. Some are so weird in shape and appearance that they have caused many people to wonder if there was some sort of evil meaning to them.

119

Once, a young man approached me with a troubled heart. According to him, his light-skinned fiancée has a strange birthmark on her back that looks a lot like the handprint of a demon burnt into the skin. He even went as far as claiming that the lady acts weird at times and he couldn't help thinking she was kind of possessed.

To solve this issue quickly and permanently, I simply showed the fellow someone related to me with a weird birthmark that covered the entire left shoulder and asked if he thought the person was possessed. He said no. Then I asked him if he really thought his fiancée was possessed now. He looked doubtful at first, then said, well, she sometimes gave him unnecessary trouble.

I actually laughed.

A day later, when I saw his fiancée and the said birthmark, I understood his worry at once. The birthmark wasn't really a handprint but could easily be mistaken for one if you kept staring at it long enough with an overactive imagination.

Birthmarks are exactly what they are, irrelevant biological blemishes on the skin and nothing more. However, in certain cases, it can be used as a unique identifier for individuals, and that is where the real danger

Rev. Ezekiel King

lies. Under certain circumstance, a demon can track a person down over vast distances just by a birthmark.

121

23. HOW DO YOU GET RID OF DEMONS IN A HOME?

Having a demon or demons in your home is one of the worst things that can happen to anyone or any family. Unfortunately, this is something that can happen all too easily and go completely unnoticed for many years as the demons wreak havoc in the lives of every member of that household, and sometimes visitors too.

Demons are fallen angels.
They are here on earth but on a
different level of existence. Hence, we
cannot see them. They hate humans
as much as humans are loved by
God. They choose to do humans
harm, cause them pain, sickness, and
destruction at every opportunity.

When a demon or demons enter into your home, they do so in three major stages.

Rev. Ezekiel King

1. The first stage is to gain complete access to a home and then overrun it.

2. The second stage is to oppress its occupants.

3. The last stage is to possess both the house and its occupants.

The ultimate goal of these demons (physically) is to cause humans pain, suffering, sickness, misfortune, internal conflict and death through suicide or accident (spiritually, their objective is to drag our immortal soul into hell). Bear this in mind as you read on.

First stage:

The first stage is that in which a demon or demons gain a foothold in your home and then overruns (or infests) it. This can occur as a result of some evil activity in the house or an attempt by someone living there to summon a demon, intentionally or unintentionally, either by the use of an Ouija board (also known as a spirit board) or a mirror, etc.

An Ouija board, also known as a Spirit board. It's an ancient object with alphabets and numbers on it, but there's more to it than meets the eyes.

This situation can happen to anyone at all and at any time. Even individuals with strong religious beliefs (such as true Christians) can have their home targeted due to some minor mistake, a careless deed or the other.

Once the demon or demons have gained full access to and overrun your home, they will then begin (the second stage) oppressing the people in that house. Everyone under that roof will be targeted, young and old.

Second Stage:

Oppression is when the demon or demons start attacking. Every family member, everyone living in that household, will experience this evil oppression. In that house, there will be constant sickness, misfortune, lack of progress, and in time, accidents and deaths (or suicides), etc. The bad news will just become so much.

In extreme cases, where the demon or demons have carved out a specific territory for themselves in that house, such as a room or a corner, the air there will be inexplicably cold, some people in the house may even feel watched, see strange lights (orbs), and have the worst of nightmares on a regular basis. There will be weird noises and occurrences around the house (which will be strongest around midnight and 3 a.m. – the hours of demons), such as banging, knocking, whispering, laughter, the malfunction of electrical gadgets, objects breaking or being moved around mysteriously, terrible odors and other such smells, the origin of which will never be found, etc. If you have pets such as dogs or even cats in that house, they will develop strange habits such as staring and growling at dark shadows or seemingly empty areas of the house or become obsessed with certain spots at which they keep scratching and growling constantly.

125

The weakest, and also, the most useful person in that family will be prime targets. The second will be hit with a crippling illness or death to bring hardship to the entire family and render it helpless, but the first will be targeted as a vessel of manipulation – demonic possession, and this is the third stage of the operation.

Note: It is important to bear in mind that the third stage of this evil operation rarely ever reaches completion. Humans can be possessed and influenced by demons, yes, but in His creation, God did not allow for complete possessions and control. Hence, it is not an easy task for demons to accomplish.

Third Stage:

Demonic possession is a situation in which a demon or demons, after systematically wearing down the defenses of a person to the point where it does not exist, then takes over the person's body. This is a complicated process that is beyond man's comprehension but well within the abilities of supernatural beings of high order. The main tools normally used by demons to wear down a person's defenses are fear, pain, lust, sleeplessness, and frustration.

Rev. Ezekiel King

- **The Fear**: Fear of darkness, fear of spirits, fear of nightmares, whatever it may be, fear is the key. It will begin with nightmares and then become reality. You will see things and hear things. You will sense the danger even if nothing is there. That fear will grow and the demons will feed on it until you finally snap and become a complete tool of evil.

- **The Sleeplessness**: You can't sleep, even at night. The restlessness will eventually get to you and your mind will be like a wide open field just waiting for anything to walk in and play around.

- **The Frustration**: You want something so badly, but can't get it, don't know how to get. The frustration will eat away at you non-stop and in the process, your defenses will fail. Eventually, when demons come with an opinion, you will jump at it without even bothering to check the consequence. Sometimes, there are no opinions and here,

127

most people do the unthinkable such as committing suicide or murder.

- **The Lust**: You will not be able to resist the incredibly powerful urges for the pleasure, fulfillment, and thrills of illicit sex and other sexual perversions. If you try, your entire system will be turned upside down and you will lose interest in everything normal or good including food. You will desire sexual gratification at all costs and it will be your undoing, spiritually and physically.

- **The Pain**: A broken, a sorrowful or the emotionally bleeding heart is a defenseless one. The door has been thrown wide open for demons to come creeping in and suicide, murder or a terrible change in character is often the end result.

Once a person's defenses have been torn down and nothing is left, demons come in to take up residence right inside that person's body and begin to do strange things.

Rev. Ezekiel King

Below are some signs to watch out for in case of demonic possession...

1. **Mental Instability**: When a member of your family, particularly a quiet and peaceful person, suddenly becomes insane in some way, in 8 out of 10 cases, you are looking at an uproar of demons in that person's body.

2. **Personality Change**: This is one sure sign that a demon has taken control of a person's body. In most cases, the person starts to talk and behave like someone with dual personality or previous lives. Look out for the constant changes of voice.

3. **Multilingual**: The possessed person will suddenly develop the ability to speak different languages, some of which are very old, e.g. Latin and ancient Greek. A lot of Christians and other religious people, hearing languages they do not understand, mistake this as speaking in tongues; a divine gift!

129

4. **Prophetic Abilities**: Believe it or leave it, some demons have prophetic abilities which are automatically passed on to their host. This is an insight into the future and things that have not yet happened. Whenever you find a mad person giving prophecies or making an attempt to do so, you are definitely looking at a possessed person.

5. **Possession of Unique Knowledge**: Due to the supernatural abilities of the demon or demons within, a possessed person will have knowledge of things that are impossible for any normal person to have, e.g. full knowledge of the secret deeds of other people.

6. **Deep-set Hatred of Religion**: Possessed people have a deep-set hatred (or fear) of religion, religious places, and items, particularly those with a touch of true holiness (Christianity). They will never go into a true church of God and holy water is pure fire to them.
    Note: Depending on the power of the possessing demon and the orientation of God's power

within an area, a possessed person may enter a church of God, but some measure of restlessness and discomfort will be apparent. The problem starts when the possessed has to approach the real holy place within that area, the holy altar, etc., or is approached by someone from there, a man of God, etc. That possessed person will react in astonishing ways, depending on what the spirit of God does to the demon or demons within them, e.g., go mad or passes out.

7. **Vileness**: One giveaway sign of a possessed person is the habit of swearing-spiting of the vilest form, and general hatred towards people,

8. **Screams**: Uttering blood chilling or unearthly screams. Possessed people are really good at this.

9. **Bizarre Reflection**: In very severe cases, the possessed person's face may have a different and very evil reflection in mirrors. The reflection may vary depending on the demon at work.

131

Command Demons with Authority

The Catholic Church is one of the oldest and most popular churches in the world today (has been for over a thousand years), but it is also one of the most useless in this situation. There have always been professional exorcists (now priests) in the Catholic church but rarely are they dispatch to help. Most times, priests dismiss the claims of demonic invasions and refuse to go help. Why? In truth, most people do not really believe in demons or the existence of a true God who created and cast them out of heaven and, going by the high rate of vile crimes in the Church today, those priests are among the unbelievers.

To so many people, demonic possessions and demons are just a figment of the imagination and so we, the affected, must protect and fight for ourselves as best as we can.

Having been a victim of these demons for so many years and now an attacker and conqueror of demons, I will help you. I will let you in on some secrets.

Rev. Ezekiel King

> ***Behold, I give unto you power
> to tread on serpents and scorpions,
> and over all the power of the enemy:
> and nothing shall by any means hurt
> you.***
>
> ***- Luke 10:19 King James
> Version (KJV)***

You do not really need a priest to rid your home or a possessed/troubled loved one of a demon. All you need is faith in God and the word of your mouth. Why? 97% of the time, the demons that take possessions of people and homes are lesser demons. They will flee once you take a firm stand against them IN THE NAME OF JESUS CHRIST.

Indeed, though the world denies it, demons know exactly who Jesus is and what he stands for. Those demons were all there when Jesus died on the cross at Calvary to save humanity from their evil grip. They all gathered at his tomb to fight to stop him from rising on the third day, but lost. Satan is still the prince of the world and his demons run riot in it, but all those who believe in God, through Christ Jesus, will be saved and live again after this world is brought to an end.

Rev. Ezekiel King

As things stand now, all you need to find shelter in the mighty power of God is to believe in Christ. Indeed, that faith alone, just calling out the name of Jesus, has saved my life countless times when, in my youth, I fought against some of the most powerful demons in existence. Demons that have tried to kill me in spirit and in reality severally; they paralyzed my body, rendered it useless in so many ways and made me insane, so I did things I never understood, all of which medical examination could not explain.

I fought, I won and I lived, but it was not by my power!

Listen. The Catholic Church and other churches who are after profit would have you believe that only certified exorcists can perform the duties of casting out demons. This is incorrect. Any Christian who knows his God, and lives a clean life, can do it and do it very well.

Begin by fasting and praying to God for one to three days and in that time, do no evil. Go to the lists of types of demons I gave you earlier in this book, write down the accompanying sin for each demon group or type and be sure to avoid them in the days of your fasting. This way, you slam shut all doors against demons. Don't forget anger and pain, and above all fear nothing.

Rev. Ezekiel King

When you are ready, pick up your Bible like a weapon and sing praise to God, then go into prayer, tell God one last time what is bothering you and ask for his power. Next, go against that demon with the necessary holy power and authority now in the words of your mouth!

Stand before the possessed person or anywhere in the troubled house and say the following words, leave no room for doubt…

IN THE NAME OF JESUS, WHO THROUGH DEATH CONQUERED DEATH AND THE WORLD, IN THE NAME OF HE WHO DEFEATED SATAN AND ALL DEMONS, I COMMAND THEE, WHATEVER YOU ARE IN MY HOME, WHATEVER YOU ARE IN MY FAMILY, WHATEVER YOU ARE IN THE BODY OF MY LOVED ONE…. LEAVE THIS PLACE NOW!!!

I, Ezekiel King, a man of God with divine authority from the living God himself tell you to use the words of this short but powerful deliverance prayer above with faith and it shall be well with you and yours.

Never beg, never plead, never fear, command and you will be obeyed.

Rev. Ezekiel King

In rare cases, where the demon or demons are so many or very powerful, particularly when they have settled in very well, driving them out can be a very difficult and lengthy task, one that will exhaust you physically and spiritually. Some cases can even drag on for years and in that time, you may make some kind of slip up on which those demons will capitalize swiftly to destroy you, their tormentor. Now you understand why it is always best to bring in a genuine man of God or an *exorcist* as the Catholic church call them, to drive out demons.

Bind Demons with Authority

Another simple method a Christian can use to get rid of demons in his or her life, family and home (thanks to Jesus Christ) is binding to render them powerless. This is good practice for demons that are deeply attached to a location or person. These types are the stubborn ones that tend to return all too quickly so do not cast them out right away – bind them first!

Go into fasting and prayers and therein, ask God for one thing repeatedly; ask him to fill you with the Holy Spirit. This is the one reason Men of God are what they are

Rev. Ezekiel King

– different from all other people; it is the divine power of the Holy Spirit in them, nothing more. God also pours out a measure of this special Spirit to anyone who so asks in the name of Jesus. It brings massive authority and power.

At the end of your prayers, you will have all power over demons and their leader Satan. The next step is to verbally and spiritually engage the demon bothering you and bind him.

Say the following words in prayer…

"Whatever demon you are, whatever Satan you may be among us (in this place), I bind you in the name of Jesus Christ to set my home and family free. I cast you out of my home, out of my family and out of my life. I send you into the pit fire where you will remain until the judgment day of God. GO NOW, QUICKLY!!!"

Tackle your problem, that demon in your home, without fear and you will be fine.

Godly Songs and Music: The Nightmare of Demons'

137

Rev. Ezekiel King

Godly songs, songs of praise unto God and Jesus Christ, are a nightmare unto demons. In fact, songs like these can be used as a very powerful weapon against them, and this, so many Christians do not know. There are too many cases where Christians fast and pray fervently over a problem for a very long time without results, but come the day, the hour, when they praise God with all their heart and strength and an amazing miracle occurs... that difficult problem is gone! Just like that!

To understand this curious phenomenon one needs to understand the very existence of the Living God and that is one of the things I spent a lot of time explaining in my book ***Creation vs Evolution***. God is a mighty king who does not stain his hands with work. He speaks and it is done; done by angels. There are hosts of powerful angelic beings, entities of God's creation, just waiting to serve him and do his bidding in all things. Each host (large group or army) has a name and duty; there are even hosts of angels specifically created to carry God's throne on their shoulders, serve, praise, and stand guard in his holy presence – the Cherubim and Seraphim! What a mighty God!

Our God, although so mighty, is also a very compassionate one where mere humans are concerned. He sees and hears all things in heaven and on earth and in people's minds. And this is one loophole that can be used to get God's blessing even in sin.

Many pray to God, but sin and a lack of faith hinder that prayer from reaching God and being answered. But come the day they dance and sing in praise to Him, even among a congregation or just a group of other Christens, and that praise will break every law in heaven to reach God's ears. If that song is pleasing unto the Lord, the angels will see that instantly and flood the venue of that praise worship to join in. Once those angels arrive, they will immediately busy themselves setting the worshipers/singers free of all problems, demonic shackles, and bondage, and then bless them in the name of the Lord, sinners and believers alike – all who are present in that place and partake in the praise worship will be blessed.

And this is one reason why some spiritual churches with gifted prophets as leaders, tend to leave the doors and windows of the church building wide open during worship - it is for the angels to enter and work among the congregation. Of course, such an action is more symbolic in nature than anything else because angels, supernatural beings that they are, do not really need doors or windows to get in and out of a building.

139

Personally, I exploit this "divine loophole" whenever I am very sad or hurt; a time when my heart is so heavy with sorrow that I cannot utter words in prayer. I sing praise to God even as I weep. My life has been full of so many trials and so I am used to doing this a lot of times. And guess what, God always knows, understands, and addresses that issues bothering my heart. This trick has never failed me and I am not alone in the use of it; apparently, Paul and Silas did just that about 2,000 years ago when they imprisoned unjustly....

16 Once when we were going to the place of prayer, we were met by a female slave who had a spirit by which she predicted the future. She earned a great deal of money for her owners by fortune-telling. 17 She followed Paul and the rest of us, shouting, "These men are servants of the Most High God, who are telling you the way to be saved." 18 She kept this up for many days. Finally, Paul became so annoyed that he turned

Rev. Ezekiel King

around and said to the spirit, "In the name of Jesus Christ I command you to come out of her!" At that moment the spirit left her.

19 When her owners realized that their hope of making money was gone, they seized Paul and Silas and dragged them into the marketplace to face the authorities. 20 They brought them before the magistrates and said, "These men are Jews, and are throwing our city into an uproar 21 by advocating customs unlawful for us Romans to accept or practice."

22 The crowd joined in the attack against Paul and Silas, and the magistrates ordered them to be stripped and beaten with rods. 23 After they had been severely flogged, they were thrown into prison, and the jailer was commanded to guard them carefully. 24 When he received these orders, he put them in the inner cell and fastened their feet in the stocks.

Rev. Ezekiel King

25 About midnight Paul and Silas were praying and singing hymns to God, and the other prisoners were listening to them. 26 Suddenly there was such a violent earthquake that the foundations of the prison were shaken. At once all the prison doors flew open, and everyone's chains came loose. 27 The jailer woke up, and when he saw the prison doors open, he drew his sword and was about to kill himself because he thought the prisoners had escaped. 28 But Paul shouted, "Don't harm yourself! We are all here!"

29 The jailer called for lights, rushed in and fell trembling before Paul and Silas. 30 He then brought them out and asked, "Sirs, what must I do to be saved?"

31 They replied, "Believe in the Lord Jesus, and you will be saved—you and your household." 32 Then they spoke the word of the Lord

Rev. Ezekiel King

to him and to all the others in his house. 33 At that hour of the night the jailer took them and washed their wounds; then immediately he and all his household were baptized. 34 The jailer brought them into his house and set a meal before them; he was filled with joy because he had come to believe in God—he and his whole household.

35 When it was daylight, the magistrates sent their officers to the jailer with the order: "Release those men." 36 The jailer told Paul, "The magistrates have ordered that you and Silas be released. Now you can leave. Go in peace."

37 But Paul said to the officers: "They beat us publicly without a trial, even though we are Roman citizens, and threw us into prison. And now do they want to get rid of us quietly? No! Let them come themselves and escort us out."

143

Rev. Ezekiel King

38 The officers reported this to the magistrates, and when they heard that Paul and Silas were Roman citizens, they were alarmed. 39 They came to appease them and escorted them from the prison, requesting them to leave the city. 40 After Paul and Silas came out of the prison, they went to Lydia's house, where they met with the brothers and sisters and encouraged them. Then they left.

*Acts 16:16-40 New International Version (NIV)

And here is yet another case in the Bible where demons are recognizing and being arrested by the superior authority of God "in the Name of Jesus Christ". Note that this demon was there in the possessed girl, following the disciples all over the place until Paul got fed with it and ordered the spirit to leave the girl's body. Until one takes a stand against these evil spirits they will stay put, keep tormenting you and never leave.

Rev. Ezekiel King

However, the issue of interest to us here is that the earthquake that occurred did so when Paul and Silas were singing songs of praise to God. The New International Version of the Holy Bible from which the extract above was pulled, uses the word 'hymns" in place of "songs of praise". Neither of these phrases refers to the **Praise/Hymn books** of today, which were made popular later on by the Catholic Church, but refer, instead, to general songs sung by the early church in praise to God.

Just singing songs of praise to God caused such amazing miracles as an **earthquake, the breaking of chains** and the **opening of locked prison gates**, all of which would never have been possible without the visit of an angel. Even the other criminals in the jail with Paul and Silas were made free too! This is the same divine loophole I am advising you use to drive out demons from your home today... all by yourself!

Playing a powerful Christian song or music loud and clear in your home, under certain conditions, with all the windows and doors in your house wide open, will do just fine. Picking the right music is the tricky part, but the following steps will guide you...

145

Rev. Ezekiel King

1. Pick a song you love, one that will move your heart, bring joy and make you sing and dance in praise to God.

2. **Pick a song that turns your heart towards God**; The Lord is where you will get your power over evil and the one with a heart that seeks Him out will be answered even in the absence of words. This is one thing I love so much about God. He listens to the heart (the mind) and the problems in it are clear to him.

3. Pick a song in which more than one person is singing. Songs by a Christian band or choir is perfect. Better still, find one in which an entire church is singing in praise to God. Always remember that where two or three are gathered god will be there in their midst. You may be doing this praise alone but the voices in the song and the light in your heart will make the difference. God will still hear you.

4. Pick a song with a lot of joy and happiness in it.

Rev. Ezekiel King

5. Pick a song that calls the name of the Lord Jesus over and over again.

6. Do not turn on your television as you play the song as this can be distracting to your mind (heart) which will be seeking out the Lord God with your problems, trying to make a connection. Instead, play the music over the sound system only... the speakers only.

7. Ensure that every door and window in that house is wide open as you play the music including the front door.

8. Ensure the music is reaching into every room. If need be, reposition your speakers.

9. If the demon or demons are troubling anyone in particular in your family, Place that person in that room in which the song is loudest, that is the room in which you should be. If possible, get your family to join you.

Rev. Ezekiel King

10. As you sing and praise God in unison with the song, let your mind connect with Him.

11. Try to do this special ritual at a time just after midnight. That is the best time – the hour of the supernatural.

Playing a joyous Christian song in your home that is in harmony with your heart and the words of your mouth directed to God will make that entire area very uncomfortable for demons, even as it is very inviting to the holy angels of God.

Without realizing it, with that ordinary song, you have turned your home into a spiritual war zone that favors only angels and the demons will know that. With the doors and windows wide open, they will rush out and get very far away from that house. Don't be surprised to see or hear sudden noises as things get damaged or moved around with violent force during this period, no one likes being forced to leave his home, least of all demons. If a door slams close, open it again. Do not be afraid, the angels of God are with you.

Rev. Ezekiel King

It is important to note that even as simple as it sounds, this process has a catch. Because they were not cast out properly but were simply forced to leave in a hurry, the demons will try to return and all too soon. In this light, it is wise to keep up this music ritual for at least 3 to 7 days.

To understand and exploit the effective timing of this ritual and other prayers, read my book *"How to Pray to God and Always Be Heard"*.

Point of Note

After the demons have left your home, pray and ask God to show you a good church to help complete that deliverance. You see, when thrown out of their home in this manner, demons tend to leave a lot of spiritual and physical mess behind, particularly if they have been in residence for a long time. A thorough spiritual and physical cleanup is called for and you certainly can't do it alone.

Additionally, it is to be noted that the use of music/songs to deal with demons is only effective with possessed houses and places. It does not always work with possessed people and that is why this topic is not mentioned anywhere else in this book. The problem here is

Rev. Ezekiel King

that possessed people, due to the demon in them, cannot praise God with all their heart and might – many of them are even hateful or scared of Godly places let alone indulge in activities there. However, if such a person can be held down in the midst of one or more people (a group or congregation of Christians) who sing and praise God in worship on the person's behalf, an answer is sure to follow.

Warning

Do not attempt to drive out any demon if your faith is not 100% solid and well rooted in Christ Jesus. Too many times, the attacker has become the attacked.

> *13 Some Jews who went around driving out evil spirits tried to invoke the name of the Lord Jesus over those who were demon-possessed. They would say, "In the name of the Jesus whom Paul preaches, I command you to come out." 14 Seven sons of Sceva, a*

Rev. Ezekiel King

> *Jewish chief priest, were doing this.*
> *15 One day the evil spirit answered*
> *them, "Jesus I know, and Paul I*
> *know about, but who are you?" 16*
> *Then the man who had the evil spirit*
> *jumped on them and overpowered*
> *them all. He gave them such a*
> *beating that they ran out of the house*
> *naked and bleeding.*
> *Acts 19:13-16*

The mistake of the men above who got dealt with by a demon is simple. They do not really know Jesus Christ only that Paul perches in his name. Well, they kept using the power in that name until the day they met a stubborn demon who questioned their authority, found them lacking and attacked.

In my opinion, that Jewish chief priest and his followers were very lucky indeed to get away with just a beating.

Also See Chapter 20: **"Who can cast out demons?"**.

Rev. Ezekiel King

Unmasking and Defeating Demons

Rev. Ezekiel King

24. MY DEMONIC PROBLEM IS COMPLEX: WILL GOD UNDERSTAND?

As long as you pray and believe, you will be amazed at how easily God will understand your situation, forgive and deliver you from even the worst of troubles.

When problems such as demonic bondage get very complex and we find ourselves in deep trouble and confusion. Many of us forget that God is very intelligent and understands the affairs of the physical and spiritual world even better than we do. Women with oppressive husbands, children with oppressive parents or guardians, Christians living in anti-Christian nations, societies or environment, yes, your oppressors may have demons in them and evil in their hearts, do they force you to worship unholy things or do evil in any manner? If you must obey to save your life or keep yourself safe from harm, do so. But keep the lord in your heart as you do that, and at any private opportunity you get, pray to him about it and worship. He will hear your cry even among sinners.

Rev. Ezekiel King

4 For if God did not spare angels when they sinned, but sent them to hell, putting them in chains of darkness to be held for judgment; 5 if he did not spare the ancient world when he brought the flood on its ungodly people, but protected Noah, a preacher of righteousness, and seven others; 6 if he condemned the cities of Sodom and Gomorrah by burning them to ashes, and made them an example of what is going to happen to the ungodly; 7 and if he rescued Lot, a righteous man, who was distressed by the depraved conduct of the lawless 8 (for that righteous man, living among them day after day, was tormented in his righteous soul by the lawless deeds he saw and heard)— 9 if this is so, then the Lord knows how to rescue the godly from trials and to hold the unrighteous for punishment on the day of judgment. 10 This is especially

Rev. Ezekiel King

> *true of those who follow the corrupt*
> *desire of the flesh and despise*
> *authority. Bold and arrogant, they*
> *are not afraid to heap abuse on*
> *celestial beings;*
>
> *2 Peter 2:4-10*

God must punish every sinner and demon worshiper even if it entails punishing an entire family, city or nation. But if even one righteous soul is to be found there, he will save that soul even as he punishes the multitudes.

155

25. CAN DEMONS RETURN AFTER BEING CAST OUT?

Yes, they definitely can, many of them do and quickly too.

In the Bible, after healing a mute man by driving a demon out of him, Jesus warns the onlooking crowds of people that unclean spirits (demons) may be cast out of a possessed person, and when they leave they will go to a waterless land and wander around, looking for other souls (people) to inhabit. A time comes when that demon, finding no new place (person) to inhabit, will return to its old home. When that demon finds that the old home has been renovated, it will go out and bring back seven more demons that are more terrible than itself and they will all enter and settle in that person. In the end, that person is in a worse condition than he was before the demon was cast out.

43 "When an unclean spirit
goes out of a man, he goes through
dry places, seeking rest, and finds
none. 44 Then he says, 'I will return

Rev. Ezekiel King

to my house from which I came.' And when he comes, he finds it empty, swept, and put in order. 45 Then he goes and takes with him seven other spirits more wicked than himself, and they enter and dwell there; and the last state of that man is worse than the first. So shall it also be with this wicked generation."

Matthew 12:43-45 New King James Version (NKJV)

The complete answer to this question is, yes, demons can and do return to their home after being cast out, but they always bring a lot of company with them. This is my experience with cases like these.

157

26. WHAT IS DEMONIC BONDAGE?

Demonic bondage is exactly what happens when an individual becomes possessed or oppressed by a demon or demons. Demons may take control of a person's life if he or she is in rebellion towards God (in sin, belief, or principle).

It takes God's discernment to ascertain which of the issues above is producing the bondage in a person's life.

When in demonic bondage, a person will suffer endlessly and nothing good comes out of the works of his or her hands. Misfortunes/bad luck, accidents, rejection, failure, these are constants in the life of someone in demonic bondage.

Rev. Ezekiel King

27. HOW DO YOU KILL DEMONS?

Because the world is full of fake preachers, ignorant people and all kinds of frauds putting out one doctrine or the other, you hear a lot of different theories on the subject of killing demons.

Once, on one of the popular social media platforms, I actually saw someone saying he had it on good authority – his church – that a demon could be killed! He went on to explain how he was taught that demons are evil (human) souls that, over thousands of years, were manipulated to become what they are... demons. He goes on to say that to kill a demon, you need to find the bones of that demon from its past life as a human and then burn them. The fellow goes on to point out that such a feat is very difficult and basically impossible given that the only entity that knows who the demon was in the past is itself,

Personally, the only thing I can say about this theory, and its origin, is that Hollywood movies have a lot more influence on people than I thought. This is exactly how people end up worshiping the wrong god all their lives; they've been going to the wrong church all along! A church where a demon is really lord and not Jesus Christ.

Rev. Ezekiel King

Demons were once angels, powerful supernatural beings that are immortals by creation. Even after their downfall and banishment from heaven, their immortality was not altered. It is what they are.

An immortal being cannot be killed, at least not by a human, a mortal being. The killing of demons is left to God who created them and understands their makeup and energy. Humans can only drive a demon or demons away from a place or an area, i.e., get rid of them, bind them and cast them into hell, in the name of God their creator and owner of all supreme power. In the past, this was done by means of elaborate rites commonly known as **exorcism**, but faith in Jesus Christ has replaced all that today.

Rev. Ezekiel King

28. HOW DO DEMONS MULTIPLY?

In the day that Lucifer, Prince of the Morning, was expelled from heaven after his rebellion, he took a third of the hosts of heaven, God's angels. Since these angels, turned demons, are immortals, they can neither multiply (reproduce) nor die and so their number remained the same for ages even till this day.

The question "How do demons multiply?" is obviously not relevant here so can be changed into "How do you invoke a demon?" You definitely don't want to do this, but in case you are fool enough to want to ruin your life in grand style then the answer to is that every single demon has a unique way it can be summoned. Usually, all that is required is knowing and speaking out the demon's real name in a specific language and under certain conditions. And this is why no matter how many times we mention or list out the names of the demons in the Bible or anywhere else, they never respond. Mentioning their name ordinarily doesn't really work. You have to speak it correctly in the right way and language.

Rev. Ezekiel King

29. CAN DEMONS KILL PEOPLE?

Yes, they certainly can, and they do it in creative ways like they have done since the beginning of the human race.

Below are some of the ways in which Demons can kill people and have been killing people for so long…

1. **Possession**: When a demon or demons possess someone, that person is normally induced into doing their bidding, which is nothing but utter evil. Demons have been leading people to commit suicide and murder in this manner for ages.

2. **Pain**: There have been too many cases in our world, past and present, where the death of a greatly beloved one triggers others, particularly in families. Rejection in love affairs has also been known to do this, the British call it the Victorian disease, a broken heart. Demons just love this sort of play out – slaughter one pig and all the others die.

Rev. Ezekiel King

3. **Stage Accidents**: Due to their ability to move things directly or induce people into doing just that, demons can cause fatal accidents that claim a lot of lives and they have been doing just that for ages.

4. **Sickness**: Not many know it, but a lot of people who die of some of the worst sicknesses of our time were actually the victims of demons who triggered it in them. I strongly believe that AIDS/HIV, given the way it came, spreads and torments humanity without a cure, is a creation of the sex demons. I also believe that if humans ever find a cure for AIDS, a worse sickness will follow swiftly.

The cases mentioned above are just the tip of the iceberg. Demons kill people in more ways than we can imagine, most of them very complex.

Their ability to kill a person who recognizes their existence and understands their way is greatly reduced. In the protection of Jesus Christ, it is almost non-existent.

Rev. Ezekiel King

Unmasking and Defeating Demons

Rev. Ezekiel King

30. WHAT IS THE SYMBOLISM OF DEMONS?

The symbolism or symbol for demons also happens to be the symbol of the religion of Satanism. It is the pentagram. To be precise, it is the one with the image of the head of Baphomet within the star. Don't forget now that Satan is the prince of demons and all evil, same thing Baphomet/the goat stood for to the Israelites in the wilderness.

Rev. Ezekiel King

The symbol of Satanism is also the symbol of all demons. Wherever you see this symbol, turn around and hurry away.

The demon (false god) known as Baphomet got its goat-like appearance (the head is in the pentagram above) from a curious event that occurred in the Holy Bible. The outcast of the unclean (or unholy) goat...

> **20 "When Aaron has finished making atonement for the Most Holy Place, the tent of meeting and the altar, he shall bring forward the live goat. 21 He is to lay both hands on the head of the live goat and confess over it all the wickedness and rebellion of the Israelites—all their sins—and put them on the goat's head. He shall send the goat away into the wilderness in the care of someone appointed for the task. 22 The goat will carry on itself all their**

Rev. Ezekiel King

sins to a remote place; and the man
shall release it in the wilderness.
- Leviticus 16:20-22 New
International Version of the Holy
Bible (NIV)

Today, Baphomet has become known as "the satanic goat" and his head appears in the middle of the symbol of demons and the Church of Satan.

Answer 2

One of the ways in which demons deceive people is by confusion (confusing the truth with half-truth and lies). They confuse people with signs and symbols that appear to come from God but isn't really so. False gods or demi-gods (demigods) are masters at this.

One such symbol demons often use here has been **the inverted/upside down cross**.

A cross is the universally recognized symbol of Christianity and the ultimate sacrifice of Jesus Christ. What

167

these demons do in some of their temples is use the same cross positioned upside down.

31. ARE CANDLES A DEMONIC SYMBOL?

No, candles are by no means demonic symbols and there is nothing specifically demonic about them. But there's a catch, and it has to do with the color of the candle.

Since ancient times, candles have been used for a lot of purposes, including religious sacrifices and rites. The practice has been there among different religions and beliefs.

The only symbol a candle stands for is that placed on it by its user or, in certain cases, anyone looking at it. It can have any meaning at all or just nothing, it's subjective. Hence, candles are used to light up homes, celebrate birthdays and even honor the dead.

However, candles are mostly used in Christian (Catholic) churches, demonic churches, and satanic rituals. White colored candles are used in churches while black or red candles are used in satanic (or demonic) rituals and worship. The black represents darkness or the Satanic world, the red is primarily demonic, while the white candles represent Godliness, purity and the light of Jesus Christ.

169

People generally use white candles in their homes and light them in remembrance and honor of dead loved ones who we want to rest in peace or go to heaven. This is a universal ritual.

32. WHY ARE THE WAYS OF DEMONS SO SIMILAR THAT OF GOD?

Demons are fallen angels whose ultimate and only goal in existence is to destroy humanity, the object of God's pleasure. One of the major ways in which they go about accomplishing this goal is by confusing and deceiving mankind. For example, where the Lord has established a religion (Christianity) and the Christian Church to save humanity through his only son, Jesus Christ, Satan has done exactly the same thing to lead humanity to hell.

While most people are aware of the existence, in society, of the religion known as Satanism and the Church of Satan, so many are not even aware that some of the nice new churches they attend daily are actually being serviced by Satan too. They think that because the pastor and leaders of the church preach from a bible and give prophecies they are legitimate servants of God. No, no, no! There is such a thing as the Satanic Bible and prophetic demons and so many pastors and church founders use both. Fame and wealth are their objectives and that is exactly what demons offer fake men of God willing to harvest souls for them.

171

So many years ago, at the tender age of 16, when my gifts and powers as a man of God were still idle, I was made exactly such an offer by a demon cloaking itself in bright green light. I refused at the time and paid a very heavy price for so many years. I later came to discover that the demon was Satan himself, the prince of demons.

The following are some of God's ways which demons have copied and use successfully to deceive people today…

1. **Religion**: Christianity is the primary religion that was divinely established on earth by Jesus Christ to bring people to God despite their sins (which are wiped away through Jesus Christ). The demonic answer to this is Satanism. Islam is another religion that is used to deceive mankind. The violence, terrorism, and bloodshed speak for themselves.

2. **The Church**: The Catholic Church is one of the oldest and largest churches on earth, but it's just one of several still doing God's work today. The answer of demons to this was to start up a host

of fake churches and cults, and top of that list is the Church of Satan with millions of worshipers worldwide!

3. **The Bible**: The Holy Book of God, for Christians, is the Bible. The demonic answer to this is the Satanic bible and different occult books.

4. **God Worship**: God, the supreme creator of all things, is the almighty onto whom all worship and praise belong. Both Christianity and Islam make this fact perfectly clear. In answer to this, many demons established themselves as gods in different lands, and have been worshiped for ages.

5. **Prophets**: A prophet is a man of God bestowed with the gift of prophecy which enables him to perform all kinds of unique tasks such as discernment and spiritual vision. In answer to this, certain demons possess people and enable them to do roughly the same thing by mixing up half-truths and lies.

173

The instances mentioned above are just the tip of the iceberg. There are simply too many ways in which demons try to emulate the ways of God in order to deceive people, but the worst of them is always that false god aspect. It is the origin of too many modern churches, cults, and different belief systems. The most famous of these false gods is the demon known as Baal or Baalrim. One of the oldest references to this demon parading itself as a god in place of the Living God can be found in the Bible book of 1 Kings 18:20-40.

Below is an extract of the story which makes an interesting read.

*Elijah and the Prophets of Baal

20 So Ahab sent to all the people of Israel and gathered the prophets together at Mount Carmel. 21 And Elijah came near to all the people and said, "How long will you go limping between two different

Rev. Ezekiel King

opinions? If the Lord is God, follow him; but if Baal, then follow him." And the people did not answer him a word. 22 Then Elijah said to the people, "I, even I only, am left a prophet of the Lord, but Baal's prophets are 450 men. 23 Let two bulls be given to us, and let them choose one bull for themselves and cut it in pieces and lay it on the wood, but put no fire to it. And I will prepare the other bull and lay it on the wood and put no fire to it. 24 And you call upon the name of your god, and I will call upon the name of the Lord, and the God who answers by fire, he is God." And all the people answered, "It is well spoken." 25 Then Elijah said to the prophets of Baal, "Choose for yourselves one bull and prepare it first, for you are many, and call upon the name of your god, but put no fire to it." 26 And they took the bull that was given

Rev. Ezekiel King

them, and they prepared it and called upon the name of Baal from morning until noon, saying, "O Baal, answer us!" But there was no voice, and no one answered. And they limped around the altar that they had made. 27 And at noon Elijah mocked them, saying, "Cry aloud, for he is a god. Either he is musing, or he is relieving himself, or he is on a journey, or perhaps he is asleep and must be awakened." 28 And they cried aloud and cut themselves after their custom with swords and lances, until the blood gushed out upon them. 29 And as midday passed, they raved on until the time of the offering of the oblation, but there was no voice. No one answered; no one paid attention.

30 Then Elijah said to all the people, "Come near to me." And all the people came near to him. And he repaired the altar of the Lord that had been thrown down. 31 Elijah

Rev. Ezekiel King

took twelve stones, according to the number of the tribes of the sons of Jacob, to whom the word of the Lord came, saying, "Israel shall be your name," 32 and with the stones he built an altar in the name of the Lord. And he made a trench about the altar, as great as would contain two seahs[a] of seed. 33 And he put the wood in order and cut the bull in pieces and laid it on the wood. And he said, "Fill four jars with water and pour it on the burnt offering and on the wood." 34 And he said, "Do it a second time." And they did it a second time. And he said, "Do it a third time." And they did it a third time. 35 And the water ran around the altar and filled the trench also with water.

36 And at the time of the offering of the oblation, Elijah the prophet came near and said, "O Lord, God of Abraham, Isaac, and

177

Rev. Ezekiel King

Israel, let it be known this day that you are God in Israel, and that I am your servant, and that I have done all these things at your word. 37 Answer me, O Lord, answer me, that this people may know that you, O Lord, are God, and that you have turned their hearts back." 38 Then the fire of the Lord fell and consumed the burnt offering and the wood and the stones and the dust, and licked up the water that was in the trench. 39 And when all the people saw it, they fell on their faces and said, "The Lord, he is God; the Lord, he is God." 40 And Elijah said to them, "Seize the prophets of Baal; let not one of them escape." And they seized them. And Elijah brought them down to the brook Kishon and slaughtered them there.

- 1 Kings 18:20-40… The English Standard Version of the Holy Bible (ESV)

Rev. Ezekiel King

This is one of my favorite parts of the Bible and I love it so much that I never tire of rereading it. The prophets of Baal obviously knew their god very well. The powerful spirit being that communicated with them constantly and gave them a position of authority and power over the people of a great nation and their king. By their hand, Baal worked "incredible miracles"; he cured illness, blessed people with wealth, children, good fortune, life, and health. Baal gave them protestation from their enemies, solved problems and delivered them from many troubles. For all these wonderful things, the people worshiped Baal as god.

The thing people fail to understand about the Living God is that most of the things mentioned above He already gave to mankind for free since the beginning of time. What the demons and their master Satan does is seize/hinder all these blessings and, in certain cases, cleverly ration or redirect it to those who they favor as "**free blessings or solutions to their problem**"!

Your eternal soul, that is the price you ultimately pay for all those nice "free" **blessings**. For allowing demons into your life, you are eternally doomed like the demons themselves, but so many never know this until it's too late.

179

And so it was that the great demon Baal reigned supreme as god in Israel for so many years. Temples were built to him and prophets served before him even as the people flocked to him. But then one day, the true God, the living God, creator of heaven and earth, came calling and the demon Baal vanished into thin air, abandoning his domain completely. But his false prophets had no idea that they had been serving a mere demon all along and so kept calling out to him in vain until Elijah put an end to their misery and stupidity by slaughtering them all at the stream dedicated to their own god. And it was on that day, the very same hour, that the Living God had mercy on Israel and ended the terrible famine in the land by sending rain in response to Elijah's prayer.

On that fateful day, in the challenge themed "*The God who answers by fire, he is God*", it was just one true prophet of God against four hundred and fifty false prophets of Baal (supported by four hundred false prophets of the demon-god Asherah), and the demons still lost.

On that day God reprimanded the children of Israel for worshipping other gods who were nothing more than idols.

There is a huge difference in the ways of God, which is the way of life and real power, and the ways of demons, which is the way of lies and death. The demons will always try to copy God's ways in order to deceive humans, but in the day of their judgment and punishment, they will be on their knees before the Living God, for he created them in the beginning and gave them license to roam the earth.

Rev. Ezekiel King

33. ARE PAGAN GODS REAL GODS OR DEMONS?

Pagan gods, fake gods, ancient gods, demigods, they are all high-ranking demons powerful enough to parade themselves as gods in order to deceive people into worshiping them and offering sacrifices. Satan himself is top of the list of this class of demons.

Many of these demons have been at this scam for thousands of years, hence, are often referred to as **ancient gods**, and trusted by many. Do not be fooled, these are demons nonetheless, and nothing good ever comes from dealing with them. Let's take a deep look at the deceptive ways in which these false gods operate.

How False Gods Work

Outlined below are the methods with which high-ranking demons set themselves up as gods. No matter the demon, it's always the same setup.

1. **Natural Leaders or Priests**: Getting a natural leader(s) or priest(s) around whom they can build their new religion, pagan belief system or cult is key. These leaders or priests are fully possessed by the demons, giving them the powers to do all kinds of amazing things in order to attract curious people and turn them in ardent followers. Fake prophets, pastors, magicians, wizards, witches, etc., this is what they really are.

2. **Followers**: By the amazing deeds of the leaders or priests, the demon will attract more and more people to itself and in time, gain a huge following of potential worshipers.

3. **The Shrine or Temple:** Now with an established religion or cult, these demons then begin to establish temples and shrines where they can be worshiped as gods and offered abominations as sacrifices. Some of these temples are even called churches today.

Rev. Ezekiel King

4. **The Miracles**: The amazing miracles these false gods work make up the center point of the whole spiritual scam thing. The Lesser demons roam the earth in legions or armies, causing all kinds of mysterious troubles, sicknesses, and misfortunes among humans. In their desperation and ignorance, the victims turn to the false prophets and priests of these demon-gods for help. These false priests and prophets perform a few amazing acts like telling the victim a bit about his past and future and then, by the power of their high ranking demon-god, orders the lesser demons causing the problem at hand to step aside. The victim is instantly free/healed, an incredible miracle no less, and you have a thankful new believer (this is the evil version of an exorcism).

5. **The Covenants and Curses**: The main way in which demons keep their followers bound to them and eventually take over their soul is by deceiving them into making seemingly 'minor' agreements or taking "oaths" that are by no means ordinary. These are actually covenants

that are binding in life and death and, when broken, invoke terrible curses that can last for generations.

All those nice **blessings** and perfect **solutions** to problems you get from demons actually put you into a covenant with them. From every human involved, a terrible payment of blood and death will be exerted in full by the demons and when not paid, the accompanying consequence/curse is terrible, and then God will punish your immortal soul in the end.

> *20 No, but the sacrifices of pagans are offered to demons, not to God, and I do not want you to be participants with demons. 21 You cannot drink the cup of the Lord and the cup of demons too; you cannot have a part in both the Lord's table and the table of demons.*
>
> *1 Corinthians 10:20-21*

Rev. Ezekiel King

And this is how the entire setup of false gods' work. It's all about demons and hidden evil and not God. Some demonic establishments can be very complex as the demons try to hide their activities from the notice of man and the living God, but their basic breakdown is not far from that outlined above.

34. WHAT IS A DEMONIC COVENANT?

A covenant is an agreement or promise; an accepted decision between two or more consenting parties. Covenants are used to establish relationships in which a promise or promises, responsibility, and punishment for any breach or breakage of that covenant is made.

Legally, covenants are better known as 'agreements' or 'deals' are binding. This sort of agreement is irreversible; a final, irrevocable commitment, a chain that locks two people together permanently.

Covenants began with the living God who first made one with Noah, and then Abraham and David; covenants that favored, first, all mankind, and next, Israel only. The new covenant in operation between God and mankind gives every single person life and authority over evil in the name of Jesus Christ only.

God is a God of covenants and one of his commandments to man is, do not make false promises. Remember now that "promise" is just another word for "covenant". No matter where a person makes it, in whatever circumstance, it is completely binding before

Rev. Ezekiel King

God, spiritually and physically, and this is the loophole demons have exploited to man's eternal injury.

A lot of people enter into demonic covenants without knowing or realizing it. The entire process is done to them deceitfully from beginning to end and demons are behind it all. This could have been accomplished while a person is in a conscious or unconscious state, but a binding demonic covenant it remains. The reality is that the devil and his demons are always on the lookout for more and more souls to devour by any and every means possible.

Below is a list of the most important things that must be present for a covenant to be binding, spiritually and physically

1. **People**: For a covenant to be binding, two or more people, or entities, must be involved. The entities can be a person, a group of people, an organization, or a spirit.

2. **Words**: Words are very important for forming a covenant, outspoken or silent, written, verbal or thought. There is a very powerful link between words and covenants.

Mere words can lock one down in a covenant, even in death.

3. **Reason**: All covenants must have a deep-lying (a very good) reason to exist and be binding or they will not be. And this is why people get away with making worthless promises each day – they have no deep-set meaning to all parties involved.

4. **Place**; The place in which you stand to utter the words of a covenant/agreement can make it binding forever. Never utter such words in a place where a demon lives or is worshipped.

5. **Blessings and Grants:** For a covenant to exist and be binding, a blessing, a good deed, item or grant must be passed from one party to the other. Demonic gods, false gods, pagan gods, are very good at offering people whatever it is they want under some certain conditions that may seem ordinary at first: a few murmured words or a simple sacrifice,

Rev. Ezekiel King

but in reality, this is a lifelong lockdown into a demonic covenant.

6. **Punishment for breaking the covenant**: For every genuine covenant broken, there is a severe punishment.

One of the reasons demons anchor their evil activities around an individual or agent such as a priest, a false prophet or magician is that they are the ones that lead other people straight into a covenant with the demon they serve. Once into such an agreement, getting out is as good as impossible because, for one thing, you have taken something you can never really return in the original form, something that belongs to an utterly evil demon… a blessing or good deed.

Broken covenants are simply deadly when they have to do with demons. This may lead to chronic poverty, sudden death, disaster, calamity, madness or childlessness in a person's life.

We are talking about a primitive trade by barter system here and that is what evil covenants are really like. When you hear a satanic priest say, if you can sleep on a grave for just two days you will be rich, or if you offer a small goat as blood sacrifice you will have children, or if you smash three white eggs beside that big tree you will be cured of your illness... you may want to take a big step back. That is a binding covenant and it with a demon.

191

35. HOW DO PEOPLE GET INTO DEMONIC COVENANTS?

People generally get into demonic covenants in very simple ways. In fact, it is all too easy for this to happen. Below are some of the way this can happen.

Adultery and Fornication

Regardless of whether you use a condom or not, a covenant is made whenever you have sex with someone who is not bound to you by marriage.

"What? Know ye not that he which is joined to a harlot is one body? For two, saith he, shall be one flesh" (1 Corinthians 6:16)

Rev. Ezekiel King

Physically, a lot of things are transferred during sex; diseases, body fluid, and even emotions. Spiritually, the same thing happens. A woman dedicated or connected to marine spirits or the shrine of a pagan god will have a great many demons in and around her. Every man that sleeps with that women will collect at least one demon. Now when that man sleeps with another girl, that demon may do her harm in some way or even invite other demons to take up residence in her body or life. The new girl moves on to other men and the circle goes on.

A man's life and destiny can never remain the same when he has illicit sex with a woman, particularly one in whom there is a demon. The first time a person has sex and the manner in which it was done, can have a heavy spiritual consequence.

Pictures or Name

Your picture or name in the hands of a heartbroken lover you made a solemn promised to marry, but later abandoned, an offended widow or anyone at all your made a promise to but never kept, can be deadly. That picture or just your name can work against you if the victim enters

Rev. Ezekiel King

into a covenant with a demon demanding vengeance against you.

Blood and Cuts

Ever wondered why some demonic cults and false gods demand that people drink blood or offer blood sacrifices to them or even make symbolic incisions (cuts) on their body. Every single one of these things is a covenant.

The case of lovers making cuts on each other and mixing up the blood with wine to drink is one of the most terrible covenants one can ever undertake. Blood covenants are the most powerful of all because there is life in the blood.

False Religion

The number of evil spiritual houses, the perversions of Satan called churches and shrines, are so many. They burn black and red colored candles, incense and even use "holy" water in worship to idols and demons. Stepping into one of these places and joining in their activities is enough to get a person into an evil covenant.

The Occult

Occult societies require all members to swear allegiance, promising that they will never ever leave the group. That oath is taken with blood and it is a powerful covenant that is binding even after death.

Food and drinks

Eating any edible item from an agent of darkness or a satanic altar can be dangerous. While foods and drinks like these may be poisonous, they rarely are. Their purpose is to quietly bind people to a demon in an evil covenant that can last for life. Parents should be careful with your kids. Witchcraft begins just like this.

Fashion

Rev. Ezekiel King

Are you a woman who loves to wear clothes that expose intimate parts of your body? Demons will love you and seek you out directly. They may even rape you as a covenant in which you have no say. The Incubus demons specialize in this type of demonization.

Rings

Demonic rings can also be repackaged as wedding rings. Put them on and you are in a covenant with a demon without knowing it.

Historically and Biblically, Jewelry has always had connections with idolatry, enchantment, spells, and charms. People put on rings for protection or good luck, for transfer of virtue, to fight or even kill. Almost every single occult society on earth has an identifying ring or jewelry which the members wear. False prophets, fake preachers and fake churches are also into this. Most rings sold in the market place today are not just for fashion anymore, but are utter evil, just waiting to connect innocent people to the demonic world without their permission or knowledge.

It's just a ring, but it could destroy your entire life and soul forever. Spiritual enslavement is guaranteed with it on your finger.

Rev. Ezekiel King

36. WHAT ARE THE SIGNS THAT DEMONIC COVENANTS ARE IN PLACE?

The following occurrences are some of the signs that indicate that there is a demonic covenant in place in someone's life.

1. **Problems That Are Resistant to Prayers**; No matter how hard or how long you pray, the problems remain in your life.

2. **Stubborn Demonic** Possessions: When there is a demon in someone or a place that bluntly refuses when commanded to depart, there is usually a hidden angle to things.

3. **Bad Habits**: When a person has a vile habit that is so difficult to break or stop. For example, addiction to drugs, alcoholism, smoking or sex, all of which is done in the worst kind of way.

4. **Rejection of God**: When you see someone reject God, the Bible or religion with a deep set hatred or even fear, that person is most likely in a demonic covenant that forbids it.

Rev. Ezekiel King

5. **Inability to Concentrate**: When someone lacks concentration even at work and there is an unexplainable disturbance deep in them, it is highly likely that the person has gotten into some sort of demonic covenant knowingly. This happens mostly when there is some good in the person that conflicts with that evil.

All of the above is the good news because it shows that a demonic covenant is in place in a person's life, but that person may still be saved. The demonic covenant is still intact, though, and has not yet been broken. The bad news begins when that convent is broken. The consequence is swift and terrible.

Death, disaster, misfortune in life, crushing poverty, childlessness, terrible accidents, and horribly complicated illnesses, these are the results of broken demonic covenants. They are curses that can be very hereditary, reaching down many generations.

Rev. Ezekiel King

37. HOW DOES ONE GET DELIVERANCE FROM DEMONIC COVENANTS AND CURSES?

Getting complete deliverance from demonic covenants and curses, even with prayers, can be very difficult if not impossible, but this is definitely a battle that can drag on for many years, particularly where the source of the problem is complicated or unknown. However, with God everything is possible and your faith can make even the most impossible things happen very quickly.

Below are some necessary steps to take in order to break demonic covenants and curse.

1. **Expose Them**: People are usually drawn into demonic covenants secretly and by trickery. One of the best and fastest ways to destroy the hold of such covenants is to expose them publicly.

2. **Confession**: Go to a true man of God or priest for confession, experience ones will advise you do it before the congregation of God's children

(the church). This is also exposure of a kind. Demonic covenants are things of darkness that are broken when brought out into the light.

3. **Begging Forgiveness**: In some of the worst cases I have ever seen which involved utter poverty and chronic sickness, the only way out for the victim was to go back and beg forgiveness from someone with whom he or she had a covenant/agreement but cheated, failed to keep or abandoned completely. This case is particularly serious where the offended victims are helpless orphans and widows; when these helpless women and children cry bitterly in oppression, a lot of spiritual beings hear it and act. Even God will not help the cursed oppressors and the only way out is to go back and beg their past victims for forgiveness. The funny thing here is that the victim (the widow or orphan who was offended) may not even know that he or she is the cause of the problem.

4. **Giving Alms to the Poor**: In cases, particularly where a party to the covenant is dead and it is

still affecting the living, giving alms to beggars and the poor can help.

In all the solutions above, fervent prayers are called for. However, things are best done with the guidance of an experienced Christian and spiritual leader. Go to a pastor or a man of God and pour out everything. Breaking demonic covenants and curses is a tricky business that, if not handled well, can swiftly result in death, and this is one reason I have not attempted to give any prayer points here.

Rev. Ezekiel King

38. WHAT IS DEMONIC TRANSFERENCE?

A demonic transference, by definition, is a situation in which the devil or a demon takes over the body of a mortal, thus making it immortal throughout the duration it inhabits the body.

Technically speaking, this is the complete fusion of a demon and human being; the demon goes into a human body and they become one so completely that the immortal status of the demon is passed on to the human body, suppressing its mortality. This ancient theory states that the host, the body in which the demon enters and fuses to, can be a human body or that of an animal.

The problem with this theory is that, not only is it so old that many haven't even heard of it, but it is one that belongs more in a Hollywood movie than in reality. This is basically the theory behind the existence of vampires.

A demon can inhabit the mortal body of a person or animal, yes. That "body" can even become resistant to a lot of things as a result, including injuries or illness, yes, but become immortal, no!

Rev. Ezekiel King

Immortality is something that lasts for all eternity and cannot be passed from one being to the other just like that. A demon or devilish spirit can inhabit a human body or that of an animal, but a time must come when that "body" must die and that demon must leave.

Answer 2

Some supernatural beings have been known to take full human form, though. In the Bible, the Lord God Almighty took on full human form in company with two of his angels on route to destroy the sinful cities of Sodom and Gomorrah. They made a stop to visit Abraham's tents where they did eat, drink and have their feet washed like very ordinary humans. When the angels got to Sodom and lodged in the house of Abraham's nephew, Lot, the men of the city even mistook them for ordinary men and demanded that Lot brought them out of his house so they could have immoral sex with them. *(Genesis 18 & 19).

All this was made possible due to a direct transformation (or transference) of immortal supernatural beings of the highest order into mortal men.

Rev. Ezekiel King

18 The Lord appeared to Abraham near the great trees of Mamre while he was sitting at the entrance to his tent in the heat of the day. 2 Abraham looked up and saw three men standing nearby. When he saw them, he hurried from the entrance of his tent to meet them and bowed low to the ground.

3 He said, "If I have found favor in your eyes, my lord, [a] do not pass your servant by. 4 Let a little water be brought, and then you may all wash your feet and rest under this tree. 5 Let me get you something to eat, so you can be refreshed and then go on your way—now that you have come to your servant."

"Very well," they answered, "do as you say."

6 So Abraham hurried into the tent to Sarah. "Quick," he said, "get three seahs[b] of the finest flour and knead it and bake some bread."

205

Rev. Ezekiel King

*7 Then he ran to the herd and
selected a choice, tender calf and
gave it to a servant, who hurried to
prepare it. 8 He then brought some
curds and milk and the calf that had
been prepared, and set these before
them. While they ate, he stood near
them under a tree.*

**Genesis 18:1-8 New
International Version (NIV)*

Another fitting example here of angels taking
human form is Jacob's physical fight with a strong man
who turned out to be an angel. And from him, Jacob
demanded blessings (Genesis 32:26)

God has also been known to do exactly the reverse
of taking full human form. This is where he transforms a
person directly from mortal state into immortality…

*5 The company of the
prophets at Jericho went up to Elisha
and asked him, "Do you know that*

Rev. Ezekiel King

the Lord is going to take your master from you today?"

"Yes, I know," he replied, "so be quiet."

6 Then Elijah said to him, "Stay here; the Lord has sent me to the Jordan."

And he replied, "As surely as the Lord lives and as you live, I will not leave you." So the two of them walked on.

7 Fifty men from the company of the prophets went and stood at a distance, facing the place where Elijah and Elisha had stopped at the Jordan. 8 Elijah took his cloak, rolled it up and struck the water with it. The water divided to the right and to the left, and the two of them crossed over on dry ground.

9 When they had crossed, Elijah said to Elisha, "Tell me, what can I do for you before I am taken from you?"

Rev. Ezekiel King

"Let me inherit a double portion of your spirit," Elisha replied.

10 "You have asked a difficult thing," Elijah said, "yet if you see me when I am taken from you, it will be yours—otherwise, it will not."

11 As they were walking along and talking together, suddenly a chariot of fire and horses of fire appeared and separated the two of them, and Elijah went up to heaven in a whirlwind. 12 Elisha saw this and cried out, "My father! My father! The chariots and horsemen of Israel!" And Elisha saw him no more. Then he took hold of his garment and tore it in two.

*2 Kings 2:5-11 New International Version (NIV)

The number of humans God has taken directly into immortality this way since the beginning of humanity can be counted on just one hand. The list begins with Enoch,

Rev. Ezekiel King

includes prophet Moses and Elijah and ended with Jesus Christ, all of whom God loved so much and showed great favor. They were humans and then they were not, for God took them directly to heaven to be with him.

What we need to understand here is that the holy God, the most powerful spirit alive, creator of all things, can do a lot of incredible things and so can his angels in whom his holy power resides. Demons, on the other hand, are fallen angels who have been stripped of their holy/godly powers and so cannot do any of these things. Nowhere in the bible has a demon ever taken full human form and they are not about to start now. The best demons can do is possess people, and this they do so well that the possessed person may take on their personality and many other demonic qualities, but immortality is never one of them.

Even sex demons, the Incubus demons, etc., who have sex with humans and impregnate women cannot and do not take on human form to do this.

Answer 3

209

Man is trichotomous in existence; he is flesh, soul, and spirit. As long as the soul remains attached to the body, that person will stay alive. The spirit may wander far and wide, such as in dreams, but it will always return to the body because the soul is still attached to it. The day the soul detaches itself from the body, that person is dead. The spirit never returns to the body after that, but becomes one with the soul and stays so forever. At this point, that person has become an immortal being or a ghost as we call the spirits of the dead.

In cases of demonic possession of humans, the demon merely suppresses the spirit and installs itself in the body as a controller. That suppression can be full or just partial, it all depends on the level of possession and the demon at work.

In that way it was not possible for the immortal soul and spirit to transfer their immortality to the body, so also is it impossible for demons to transfer their own immortality to that body;

Demons may change the characteristics or abilities of the body they inhabit, but inducing total immortality for any length of time is not an opinion.

Rev. Ezekiel King

39. WHAT IS DEMONIC INFLAMMATION?

A very rare occurrence indeed, but this is a situation where a person has been scratched or physically marked by a demon. It is said that when this happens, the victim feels a burning sensation at the spot, and the inflamed or reddened area bears claw marks or offensive or shocking wording.

Trees, houses, and other animals can also be marked by demons. It's all about inspiring fear and confusion in human beings nothing more.

40. WHAT FOOD DO DEMONS EAT?

According to Hollywood movies and general superstition, demons feed on human flesh, blood and souls. Unfortunately, this is a very wrong assumption. For instance, how many cases of 'demonic' half-eaten human bodies have been reported since prehistoric times? We are talking about a huge number of terribly hungry demons here, there has to be some leftover food somewhere in all the time that has passed since the creation of mankind.

All those Hollywood movies about vampires and demons eating humans have got a lot of people confused about the real demonic creatures.

Demons, immortal beings that they are, do not, and cannot, feed on the flesh or blood of mortals. They cannot eat human souls either because those are immortal beings in their own right.

23 May God himself, the God of peace, sanctify you through and through. May your whole spirit, soul and body be kept blameless at the coming of our Lord Jesus Christ.

Rev. Ezekiel King

1 Thessalonians 5:23 New

International Version (NIV)

What demons feed off is fear! Human fear.

The more a person fears a demon, the stronger and more powerful the demon grows. That fear is the food causing that growth. Take that fear away and you have a starved demon that can do you no harm.

Sins merely open the door for demons to enter one's life or body, not feed them.

So Why Are Demons So Crazy About Getting People's Souls?

Demons are so desperate to get (steal) the souls of human beings because they are the ultimate prize in the massive demonic campaign of spiting the Living God, their creator.

Of all God's creations, humans are the most beloved by Him and demons the most despised (rejected) due to their terrible sin. Demons know exactly where they stand with God and their final punishment of hell. Their ultimate goal then is to take as many humans as possible along with them to hell and the immortal form of humans are souls. Thus, demons aim to capture the souls of people, not their body which is just flesh and blood that must perish. At death, the soul and spirit of a person leave his body and become one immortal being known as a spirit or ghost.

41. WHAT DOES DEMONIZE MEAN?

To demonize someone, in the human sense, is the same thing as to portray that person as evil to others, a source of evil or threatening in a sinister manner.

Demonizing people, particularly when they are innocent, is very wrong and wicked. Such an act can change a person's life for the worse, portray them in the wrong light to society and, in extreme cases, lead to suicide. The group/type of demons that lead people to do things like this are known as (false) Accusers.

Do not liken a person to a demon or devil under any circumstance.

Answer 2

In some cases, the term "demonize" is also used in reference to people who have been possessed by demons. Hence, the reference to their being evil.

215

42. WHAT IS A DEMONIC OPERATOR?

In the world of magic, a demonic operator is believed to be a ghost or spirit being from the supernatural world that helps a magician perform his or her act successfully.

A lot of magicians believe that there is nothing evil about these spirit helpers and some will even tell you that those spirits are gentle or friendly. Unfortunately, there is no such thing as a gentle or friendly about these particular group of spirits or ghosts. In fact, the immortal spirits of the dead, have very limited abilities and cannot really help magicians in any major way. However, a demon can!

Interestingly, demons constantly fool people into thinking they are gentle, co-operative or friendly spirits. They even pretend to be ordinary ghosts a lot of times. Let me share a strange story with you. A personal experience…

"Many years ago, when I was about 13 years old, on my way back from school one afternoon, I came across a magician who had set up shop by a popular bus stop. A crowd had gathered to watch the magician perform and I joined them. Note that this is what magicians do when they want to attract followers and customers who would require their services in some way and then make a commitment. As I watched, the magician performed a lot of wonders, making things disappear and plucking wads of money right out of thin air. Of all his acts only one really had me shaken.

It occurred when the magician dropped a large cow horn on the ground and invited six strong men from the crowd of onlookers to come forward and pin it down. The men stepped forward and obeyed. Six big men, they held that cow horn down on the ground with both hands, leaning on it with all their weight and strength.

The magician took a few steps backward from the group of men, squatted and, with a few murmured words, hit the bare ground with the flat palm of his open hand and kept it there.

Like something out of a horror movie, that cow horn leaped right off the ground, lifting the six men with it. The men fought to keep it down but couldn't, they weren't strong enough, and the horn kept elevating until it was at about waist level.

Suddenly, without warning, the magician took his flat hand off the ground and that cow horn fell to the

217

ground lifelessly. The six men fell right on top of it and on top of each other.

The men scrambled to their feet quickly and scattered in fear. Four of them headed off down the road at a full run as if something terrible was pursuing them!

The magician roared with laughter and then asked who and who among the crowd wanted power like that. Several other men stepped forward at once!"

And that was the day I started wondering about life, the spirit world and the powers that be in it.

Make no mistake, ghosts or spirits of the dead cannot help magicians in any real way. Demons are the ones that work the art of magic.

Rev. Ezekiel King

43. WHO CREATED DEMONS?

The Lord God Almighty, he who was in the beginning, creator of the heavens and the earth and all that is in them, he created the beings known as demons.

In the beginning, God created the demons as angels of heaven, powerful supernatural entities of holiness and purity, and Satan was above them all.

Satan's original name as an angel was Lucifer, prince of the morning. He had more authority and power in heaven, even than the archangels, for he was a prince, second only to God and his son Jesus Christ. And there came a day when the sin of jealousy and greed entered into the heart of Lucifer and he decided he wanted to take the place of God, the supreme ruler of all things.

Lucifer was the mightiest of all the angels in the kingdom of Heaven. He was third in line from God in authority and chief of the four powerful archangels who were captains over the entire host of the angels of Heaven. Only God himself

219

Rev. Ezekiel King

and His son were above Lucifer and Lucifer had the power to rule in God's name. And that was the way in which he won the hearts of so many angels.

Now, all the angels were created with the knowledge of good and evil, but at the beginning, when they all served the Lord God, they were all good, even like the Lord. But a time did come when Lucifer, Prince of the Morning, having grown too proud, rebelled against his God; and the number of angels that stood with him that day was a third of the number of all the angels in the kingdom of Heaven.

And the Son of God went and stood before His Father, seeking permission to war against Lucifer, but God gave him not that permission, for his name was peace.

And next came the Archangel Michael to bow before the throne of

Rev. Ezekiel King

God. He was the chief and the most powerful of the four Archangels, he who never tolerates a sin against God and punishes such with great vengeance. Michael stood before the Lord God and asked permission to war against Lucifer and his angels. And the Lord granted him full permission, for his name was war and he tolerated no sin against God.

(Creation vs Evolution by Rev. Ezekiel King).

The extract above is from one of my books "Creation vs Evolution". Below is a corresponding extract from the Holy Bible.

7 And war broke out in heaven: Michael and his angels fought with the dragon; and the dragon and his angels fought, 8 but they did not prevail, nor was a place found for them in heaven any longer.

221

Rev. Ezekiel King

> *9 So the great dragon was cast out,*
> *that serpent of old, called the Devil*
> *and Satan, who deceives the whole*
> *world; he was cast to the earth, and*
> *his angels were cast out with him.*
> *(Rev 12:7-9 ...NKJV)*

God created angels only, but sin caused demons to become.

44. CAN DEMONS TOUCH YOU?

Yes, demons can definitely touch humans but do not expect that touch to feel a lot like a human touch. Demons are supernatural beings of evil and nothing good comes of their touch.

Paralysis, sickness, misfortune, madness; it will amaze many to know that the mere touch of a demon can result in these cases.

A demon can touch a human being and also possess them. But always, it is to the injury of that person.

223

45. CAN PEOPLE FEEL THE PRESENCE OF DEMONS?

Apart from people specifically blessed with the gift of spiritual awareness, no ordinary person can feel or sense the presence of a demon. For one thing, they don't even know the exact signs to look out for in such circumstances.

However, the human body does have an immortal soul present within it and this can be an advantage in certain cases. Depending on a person's level of alertness, spiritually and physically, that person can feel "uneasy in certain areas", feel watched, or even feel chills of sorts in the presence of spirit beings. This often happens when that person is alone and all his or her senses are on full alert to find something, usually another person hiding somewhere or other. You are looking for one thing, but your hyper-alert senses are detecting another which you don't even understand.

When I was younger and very much **an ordinary person**, I used to have all these sensations at odd periods and places, particularly during hours of darkness. The most common of them was a strange kind of shiver running down my back, beginning from my head. It took me a long time to figure out that I was being watched or in the presence of a demon or a supernatural being.

Answer 2

Sometimes you will hear people say they feel a presence within them that makes them stronger, faster or smarter, etc. That's a person possessed by a demon, there's nothing ordinary about him or her. If you are close to such people, look for these signs...

1. Change in personality or voice.
2. Eloquence in more than one language
3. Talking strangely (sometimes to no one).
4. Avoiding eye contact

If you spot any of these signs, do not confront them about it. Go away and stay away. However, if someone you love or a relative is the victim, then you have a very serious problem on your hands.

Rev. Ezekiel King

46. WHAT IS THE TIME OF DEMONS?

In the correct order of things in the world, the "time of humans", the time at which humans are most active, is generally known as "daytime". This period generally stretches from sunrise to sunset. However, modernization has allowed man to effectively extend that time to about midnight.

Depending on who you ask, the time of demons may vary. Midnight and 1 a.m. are the answers you will hear the most. The correct time of demons (the time they are most active), however, is much broader than that.

The time of demons begins at about an hour before midnight (11 p.m.). From that time till about one hour after midnight is a demonic period known as the "watch hour". Demons are most active from 1 a.m. to about 3 a.m.

It is interesting to note that in most ancient cults, 3 a.m. is known as the devil's hour and sacrifices are made during that period.

One Clear Proof of the Goal of Demons on Earth

Rev. Ezekiel King

For those who doubt that the ultimate goal of demons is to destroy humanity, you are looking at clear proof right here. Ask yourself just a few simple questions...

1. **Question**: At what time is the human body weakest?

Answer: Between 1 a.m. and 3 a.m. when a person is in deep sleep.

2. **Question**: At what time is the human body completely defenseless?

Answer: Between 1 a.m. and 3 a.m. when a person is in deep sleep and unconscious.

3. **Question**: At what time are demons most active?
Answer: Between 1 a.m. and 3 a.m.

4. **Question**: Why on earth would an evil creature be most active at such a time.
Answer: To exploit human weaknesses to the full.

A mosquito is most active at night when it can suck blood freely from sleeping people. An owl is most active at night because its preys come out at that time to hunt for

Rev. Ezekiel King

food. A demon is most active at night because its prey, humans, are most defenseless at that time and so it can do its evil work on them freely.

47. WHAT IS A SMALL DEMON CALLED?

Demons are demons and there is no such thing as a small or big sized demon. What demons have to separate them in nature is rank and power. Satan, the highest ranking demon, is also the most powerful and all the other demons that pass themselves as gods fit in just below him in authority and power. High ranking demons have authority over lesser demons who roam the earth in legions or armies.

Man has a way with words and since ancient times, some have always thought of demons coming in big and small sizes. The name given to a small sized demon is an imp.

Rev. Ezekiel King

48. WHAT POWERS DO DEMONS HAVE?

Demons are supernatural beings with a lot of power and they are capable of doing things far beyond human comprehension. They can possess and control human beings or animals, manipulate them by filling their minds with thoughts and uncontrollable urges, induce superhuman strength and speed, drain energy, move around as shadows or completely invincible beings and much more. Some demons have even been known to use mirrors as gateways to move from place to place.

However, their greatest and most effective power has always been deception. The ability to thoroughly convince man that they do not exist.

*See also question 9 (What can demons do?) and question 2 (Do demons really exist?).

49. DO DEMONS EAT OR KILL SOULS?

A lot of Hollywood movies depict demons as eaters or killers of souls. They even go a step further to portray them as eaters of flesh and drinkers of blood (sometimes as vampires). All these things exist only in the movies and are of great profit to moviemakers.

Demons do not, cannot and will never be able to eat or kill the souls of human beings, which are as immortal (cannot be killed) as they are. A soul is actually an independent entity, a human being in its immortal state and so certainly can't be 'eaten' up by another immortal entity. God did not make things that way.

Additionally, demons cannot and do not eat flesh and blood.

So why are demons so obsessed with stealing souls? It is their prize. It is their ultimate goal to take as many souls as possible with them into hell in order to spite God who loves humans so much.

Rev. Ezekiel King

50. WHERE IS THE MAIN HOME OF DEMONS?

The answer most Christians will give here is "hell" and they won't be too far from the truth. However, a good read of the Bible shows that demons have been "*going up and down in the earth and wandering around in it*" for ages without a fixed location as a home or city.

> *6 One day the angels[a] came*
> *to present themselves before the*
> *Lord, and Satan[b] also came with*
> *them. 7 The Lord said to Satan,*
> *"Where have you come from?"*
> *Satan answered the Lord,*
> *"From roaming throughout the*
> *earth, going back and forth on it."*
> *8 Then the Lord said to Satan,*
> *"Have you considered my servant*
> *Job? There is no one on earth like*
> *him; he is blameless and upright, a*
> *man who fears God and shuns evil."*

Rev. Ezekiel King

9 "Does Job fear God for
nothing?" Satan replied. 10 "Have
you not put a hedge around him and
his household and everything he has?
You have blessed the work of his
hands, so that his flocks and herds
are spread throughout the land. 11
But now stretch out your hand and
strike everything he has, and he will
surely curse you to your face."
12 The Lord said to Satan,
"Very well, then, everything he has is
in your power, but on the man
himself do not lay a finger."
(Job 1: 6-12 NIV)

Demons have no specific home and are condemned to wander the earth until the day of their judgment. That is their divine punishment for now. If you have a good read of the Bible you will understand that "hell" or the "lake of fire" is a place made ready to receive and torment demons for all eternity after the judgment day. While some demons are already imprisoned there, most are not. They are free to roam and that roaming is done majorly on earth here.

The Bible book of Revelations agrees that most demons are here on earth, but locked away underneath the Euphrates River until they get released in Armageddon.

When one takes the words of the Book of Revelations literarily and considers the incredible number of demons roaming free on earth, inflicting sufferings and wreaking havoc on humanity, that person may begin to imagine that at some point in time there was some sort of a massive jailbreak by the demons under the Euphrates River! The thing to understand about the Book of Revelations is that it is a book of visions (prophetic revelations to a seer); predictions of the future, clarification of God's will and laws, all done by symbolism and not reality. For example, Satan, prince of all demons, is often portrayed as a great dragon in the Book of Revelations. As we all know, dragons do not exist on earth.

Rev. Ezekiel King

51. WHY DO DEMONS HAUNT PEOPLE?

In 80% of cases involving people, houses or an area being haunted by a ghost, what you are looking at is impersonation on a supernatural level, a demon playing out the life of someone who died in some kind of sin. Ghosts do exist, but not to torment people that way.

Demons haunt houses, places or people in order to reach through to the real world, take a foothold in it, and connect with the living. Impersonating the spirits of dead people to do this is just a demon's smart way of taking a short cut to its goal.

A person will readily open up or surrender to the spirit of a dead relative, friend, hero or historical figure more than anything else. Where the ghost is famous (i.e., one that is widely known to appear constantly or periodically in a particular place) or violent, people are overcome with fear and the demons feed off that fear.

Demons haunt people to get access to their life, body, and, ultimately, their soul.

Also See Chapter 45: **Are Ghosts and Demons the Same?**

Rev. Ezekiel King

Unmasking and Defeating Demons

Rev. Ezekiel King

52. WHAT IS AN INNER DEMON?

An inner demon is merely another way in which people say "You are your own worst enemy"

If you've got the constant urge or a tendency to do something that is directly or indirectly damaging to your person, even in the presence of good advice and personal awareness of the harm being done, then it can be said that you are your own worst enemy. This is tantamount to having an **Inner Demon**. It is exactly what happens to possessed people; they do themselves harm.

Answer 2

An inner Demon may also be referred to as something you think about so much. For example, if you once attempted to save the life of an accident victim, but failed, then the incident can haunt you for a very long time indeed. It will end up becoming your "inner demon".

Rev. Ezekiel King

53. ANGELS AND DEMONS, WHICH ARE MORE POWERFUL?

This is one question that almost every Christian would love answered, but many cannot answer satisfactorily - which is the more powerful of the two supernatural beings, angels or demons? Luckily, Hollywood has got things somewhat right this time with their endless movies about angels and demons, but there is more to it than meets the eyes.

In the beginning, Satan was the highest ranking angel in existence, second only to God and his son Jesus Christ, right up to the day he sinned, was defeated in war, and cast out of Heaven. The angel that defeated Satan in that heavenly war and kicked him out of Heaven was the archangel Michael

The Bible makes us understand that, in sin, Satan took a third of the angels of heaven with him and they were all kicked out of heaven together.

7 And war broke out in heaven: Michael and his angels

Rev. Ezekiel King

fought with the dragon; and the dragon and his angels fought, 8 but they did not prevail, nor was a place found for them in heaven any longer. 9 So the great dragon was cast out, that serpent of old, called the Devil and Satan, who deceives the whole world; he was cast to the earth, and his angels were cast out with him.

*Revelations 12:7-9 (NKJV)

****

4 His tail swept down a third of the stars of heaven and cast them to the earth. And the dragon stood before the woman who was about to give birth, so that when she bore her child he might devour it.

Revelations 12:4 (ESV)

239

Due to that sin and banishment from heaven, Satan was stripped of his lofty position, authority and holy power, but retained a lot of power as a supernatural being of high order as did all the demons who were with him.

It is that supernatural power of demons, still being great in itself, that enables them to put up formidable resistance against angels in certain ways. A lot depends on the rank of that angel and the demon it is up against. However, no demon can stand against the archangels and Archangel Michael is the chief and most powerful of them all. His name is war and he tolerates no sin against God.

Below is the account of an angel sent with a message to Daniel as narrated in the old testament of the Holy Bible.

> *11 He said, "Daniel, you who are highly esteemed, consider carefully the words I am about to speak to you, and stand up, for I have now been sent to you." And when he said this to me, I stood up trembling.*
> *12 Then he continued, "Do not be afraid, Daniel. Since the first*

Rev. Ezekiel King

day that you set your mind to gain
understanding and to humble
yourself before your God, your words
were heard, and I have come in
response to them. 13 But the prince
of the Persian kingdom resisted me
twenty-one days. Then Michael, one
of the chief princes, came to help me,
because I was detained there with the
king of Persia.

> **Daniel 10:11-13 The New*
> *International Version (NIV)*

In the verses above, we see that an archangel is referred to as a "chief prince." The angels are princes and so are demons. Angels are spiritual prices of holiness and heaven while demons are spiritual princes of evil and the world.

The Holy Bible warns that Christians do not battle against flesh and blood; but rather, **"against principalities, against powers, against the rulers of the darkness of this world, against spiritual wickedness in high places"** **(Ephesians 6:12)**. These are demons in action, already well

Rev. Ezekiel King

established among humans in the world. To displace them, angels have to fight or go to war and where the more powerful archangels are not involved, that war can drag on for quite a while. And this is one reason why nowhere in the Holy Bible are humans advised to call out to angels or rely on them for effective deliverance from demons, but rather, are told to believe in the power of God, through Jesus Christ and they will be saved! The key is the authority Jesus Christ holds alongside his father, the Living God. That power and authority are far greater than that of an archangel, angel or demon, therefore, must be obeyed.

Answer 2

Of all the angels currently in existence, the four archangels are the strongest and, Archangel Michael is the strongest and most powerful of those four. He is the general in charge of war before the Living God and commands the armies of Heaven. He does not tolerate sin against God and punishes such swiftly with death. It was Archangel Michael that God made guardian angel over Israel in the day He led them out of the land of Egypt, which is why no adversity

Rev. Ezekiel King

could stand before them, human or demon, and whenever
they sinned, so many died

> **20 "Behold, I send an Angel**
> **before you to keep you in the way and**
> **to bring you into the place which I**
> **have prepared. 21 Beware of Him**
> **and obey His voice; do not provoke**
> **Him, for He will not pardon your**
> **transgressions; for My name is in**
> **Him. 22 But if you indeed obey His**
> **voice and do all that I speak, then I**
> **will be an enemy to your enemies and**
> **an adversary to your adversaries.**
> ***Exodus 23:20-22 The New**
> **King James Version (NKJV)**

God may forgive sins endlessly, but some
archangels obviously don't.

Below is a spectacular playout of a battle involving
the Archangel Michael and a king who places his trust in
false gods whom, as we now know, are merely high
ranking demons.

243

This story is rather interesting and possesses a lot of historical and religious value. It begins with the Egyptian king's refusal to let the enslaved Israelites leave his land as demanded by Moses, the chosen messenger of God. After Egypt had been hammered by several plagues, including a terrible Passover by an angel which killed every first-born child in the land and punished every "god", Pharaoh finally let God's children go only to change his mind shortly afterwards and pursue after them within his entire army. His aim? To kill them all.

The Egyptian army finally found the defenseless Israelites camped by the Red Sea on their way into the desert and made ready to attack them at once. The children of Israel cried out to Moses, their leader, in fear and Moose cried out to God in turn. Below was what happened next…

15 The Lord said to Moses, "Why do you cry to me? Tell the people of Israel to go forward. 16 Lift up your staff, and stretch out your hand over the sea and divide it, that the people of Israel may go through the sea on dry ground. 17 And I will

Rev. Ezekiel King

harden the hearts of the Egyptians so that they shall go in after them, and I will get glory over Pharaoh and all his host, his chariots, and his horsemen. 18 And the Egyptians shall know that I am the Lord, when I have gotten glory over Pharaoh, his chariots, and his horsemen."

19 Then the angel of God who was going before the host of Israel moved and went behind them, and the pillar of cloud moved from before them and stood behind them, 20 coming between the host of Egypt and the host of Israel. And there was the cloud and the darkness. And it lit up the night[b] without one coming near the other all night.

21 Then Moses stretched out his hand over the sea, and the Lord drove the sea back by a strong east wind all night and made the sea dry land, and the waters were divided. 22 And the people of Israel went into the

Rev. Ezekiel King

> *midst of the sea on dry ground, the*
> *waters being a wall to them on their*
> *right hand and on their left.*
> **Exodus 13:17-15:22 The*
> *English Standard Version (ESV)*

As you have seen, at the cry of Moses, God question why he does that when he already has **"power"** right there with him. That power was the Archangel Michael. Notice how the archangel moves swiftly to block the armies of Egypt and then splits the Red Sea? God is king. He sits on his throne and the angels, with his mighty power and authority in them, serve him.

An angel can do battle with several demons and emerge the victor, but when up against very high ranking demons like the devil himself, who was once at a higher level than them, they struggle and must have help from other angels. Archangels, on the other hand, can do battle with all manner of demons and win single-handedly. Archangel Michel is the most powerful of all.

In the ***Testament of Solomon***, the secret behind King Solomon's ability to enslave several powerful demons to help build his temple was a ring given to him by the archangel Michael.

Another interesting fact here is that one of the powerful demons enslaved by Solomon was summoned from the bottom of the Red Sea. He revealed himself to Solomon as Abizithibod, one of the demon gods of Egypt. This Red Sea demon revealed that it was he who supported the magicians of Egypt against Moses, he who hardened the heart of Pharaoh against Israel and made him pursue after them even into the Red Sea.

Abizithibod claimed that he had been caught with the armies of Egyptian when the sea closed up over them and was pinned down by a mighty pillar.

Apparently, the Archangel Michael, fed up with the activities of this demon in hindering the Children of Israel, dropped a massive pillar on him, pinning him down at the bottom of the sea.

Abizithibod told Solomon that the pillar had held him down since that time until Ephippas (another demon enslaved by Solomon) came and together, they both lift the pillar.

What we have here is a demon held down by a pillar at the bottom of the sea for centuries! A demon that needed help to lift a pillar dropped on him by an archangel.

247

Rev. Ezekiel King

With the help of another powerful demon, the Red Sea demon was able to free himself at last and together, both demons brought the pillar to Solomon.

Solomon describes the pillar as a "miraculous" structure of purple.

54. CAN DEMONS STALK YOU?

Yes, demons can and do stalk a lot of people. Unlike human beings who have little patience, demons can keep at this for years as they wait and watch for loopholes in a person's life or whatever else it is they want.

Usually, demons do this when they have some kind of interest in someone or when a person has summoned them by mistake or in ignorance. Men of God are usually stalked and, from my experience, so are Christians or good people with some kind of special destinies.

Rev. Ezekiel King

55. WHAT COLOR ARE DEMONS?

By this question, we are not referring to the complexion of the skin of demons or anything like that, but the color of the light of their presence. Supernatural beings of high order have this characteristic.

For prophets and "seers" with the gift of spiritual vision, a supernatural being can be identified instantly by the light of its presence. Most of these beings never even reveal their actual self, it's just that unique light from within which their voice can be heard.

If you read the Bible carefully, you would realize, from the accounts of many holy prophets, that the light of God's presence is a dazzling bright white light which can be blinding when looked at directly. It is just like the sun in quality, but much brighter, completely pure and definitely not hot.

16 The dazzling light of the Lord's presence came down on the mountain. To the Israelites the light looked like a fire burning on top of the mountain. The cloud covered the

Rev. Ezekiel King

> *mountain for six days, and on the*
> *seventh day the Lord called to Moses*
> *from the cloud.*
> **Exodus 24:16*

Angels also have the same appearance, the bright white light of their presence, but it's never quite the same as that of the Most High God, whose light is so powerful that he cloaks himself in clouds when coming near mortal man.

Demons, having lost their holiness, are cloaked in darkness (utter blackness), not light. Out of that darkness is where their voice comes from and, yes, where they appear to come from. However, some high ranking demons that pass themselves off as gods often portray themselves gloriously to fool people. The most common color the light of the presence of these demons take on is a vibrant red which actually represents Hell, but others do appear in lights of different colors.

Some authoritative Christian figures have the theory that the color of the light of the presence of some high ranking demons represent the sin they stand for. However, I strongly disagree.

251

Why?

As I mentioned earlier in this book, I once had an encounter with Satan himself many years ago when I was very much ordinary. The light of his presence was green; the same color as the forests and plants of the earth. Green represents the fertility of the earth more than anything else.

Rev. Ezekiel King

56. ARE THERE NICE DEMONS?

There is no such thing as a nice or good demon, but there is such a thing as a deceptive demon and all demons are very clever.

Note now that there is a world of difference between lower spirits and demons. Lower spirits are the ghosts of dead people, such as loved ones, who have passed on and they are generally nice, will never do you harm, and reside in a place of rest as God made it. Demons, on the other hand, are spirits of a higher level of existence that are pure evil in nature and never rest in their activities. (See Also: Are Ghosts and Demons the Same?)

Many demons use offers such as cure to illnesses, vengeance against one's enemies, the gift of wealth, and solutions to impossible problems, to lure and deceive people into thinking they are nice and wish to help. Demons that portray themselves as gods to be worshipped are very good at this deception and what they never tell you is that acceptance of their help in any manner, places your entire life and immortal soul in their hands. This is demonic covenants and curses in the making.

Rev. Ezekiel King

These demons are nice until the day comes when they demand a terrible price of the worshipper or follower. Until you hear the terrible story of someone forced to commit dehumanizing acts of abomination such as incest or the murder his own mother, father, wife, child or relative (sometimes the entire family) as a sacrifice to one of these 'nice' demons you will never understand the level of evil/wickedness we are dealing with here. Terrible death is the consequence that follows any refusal to obey a demon after it has done you a service which placed you firmly in its debt. This is a demonic covenant, you must pay heavily or die; your children, grandchildren, and great-grandchildren will even pay (I have seen this too many times – the sin of a forefather affecting an innocent descendant). Once in this position, nothing can really save you because you are cursed by demon and rejected by God. So be very careful in the agreements you make, intentionally or otherwise, when dealing with any spirit or human.

Rev. Ezekiel King

57. WHAT DAYS ARE FORBIDDEN TO DEMONS?

There is no such thing as a forbidden day or days to or for demons and there is no such thing as taking time off from their work of destroying humanity. Even God rested on the seventh day and blessed that day to be holy, but there is no such thing for demons.

Demons are restless and lawless beings with a lot of evil energy to spread around. There is no rest day for them and no law on earth can hold them back from conducting their machinations on humanity day and night, every day and all year long.

Demons can hit anyone at any time or place, even when the person is asleep or resting on a Sunday.

Rev. Ezekiel King

58. ARE GHOSTS AND DEMONS THE SAME?

Demons and ghost are not the same and never will be the same. In fact, they are very different from one another.

Ghosts are the immortal spirits of dead people. Usually, they stay well away from human beings and hardly ever interfere with anything in the physical world. They exist at the lowest level in the supernatural realm and are very limited in power and authority. In fact, according to the will of God, the spirits of the dead exist in a place/state of rest until the day of judgment.

Demons, on the other hand, though supernatural beings as well, are far more powerful than mere spirits or ghosts. They are pure supernatural evil. Demons can take the form of ghosts to haunt the living, but ghosts cannot take the form of demons in any way.

Many ignorant people mistake ghosts for demons and vice versa.

See Also: **Are Demons the same as Evil Spirits?**

Rev. Ezekiel King

Ghosts, the Dead, and Hauntings

In some rare cases, depending on how an individual dies the ghost can be shut out of that place of rest, temporally or permanently. Ghosts like these have been known to stick around the living and even do them harm by way of their supernatural abilities.

Great emotion such as anger, sorrow or fear have been known to cause this in the spirits of dead people. Certain covenants also do this. When you hear a ghost is haunting a place, a house or a person and it is real, the issue is not far from one of these things. So how does one solve this bizarre problem?

If it is a covenant involved, the ghost needs to be released from it to have rest. Find the second party involved in that covenant to release the dead person by just speaking words to that effect or get a powerful man of God with authority to do it.

In cases where powerful emotions are binding a ghost to the world of the living, the fastest way to solve the problem is to get a loved one or a relative of the dead person (or ghost) was very much attached to and have them speak to it with authority and send it to rest. A man of God

257

can do this too by way of his divine authority, but personally, I would rather use a loved one to send the ghost away to rest, for it has suffered enough.

To find out what is wrong with spirits like these a servant of God with the gift of spiritual awareness/vision can be of great help. The other opinion is for a loved one or relative to ask the spirit directly in dream with the help of prayers. Are you the affected one? Do the following.

*Pray to God at about midnight for help and protection, and then, mention the full name of the ghost involved authoritatively three times and demand answers for its actions in the name of Jesus Christ. As you do this, keep thinking about that dead person as you remember him or her in life and this will program your mind and spirit in a way you can never understand. If you get this process right, once you go to sleep, your spirit will seek out that ghost in the spirit world and that ghost will be doing the same thing. Both of you will eventually meet and all the questions in your mind will be answered automatically. The Lord's power will protect you at every step and no evil will hurt you. *

Life is a very terrible and complicated place to be and man doesn't know the half of it.

Rev. Ezekiel King

59. ARE GHOSTS AND DEMONS AFFECTED BY SALT OR FIRE?

Standing and watching a burning building or house, what you see is people running in and out, trying to save lives and as much valuable property as they can. This is not so with spirit beings such as ghost or demons. That physical fire that harms man, who is flesh and blood, has no effect on spiritual beings. The only fire that can harm spiritual beings, the one that scares demons so much, is the eternally tormenting fire of the living God and that is what awaits them in that place known as hell.

Another thing to note here is that, when a person dies, regardless of the place or circumstance, even if it's in the middle of a terrible inferno, the person's spirit lingers around the corpse for a while, completely unhurt, before it departs for good.

Physical things are not effective against spiritual beings. Earthly fires are very physical.

As for Salt, it does not do demons any harm whatever, though there are those who believe differently. A case that can be made here is that there is an entire group of demons that have built a whole kingdom at the bottom of

Rev. Ezekiel King

the sea – the marine spirits. Seawater is very salty indeed and yet these demons live there.

Rev. Ezekiel King

60. HOW HOT IS HELL?

One of the things that terrify demons so much is the prospect of going to hell. I am yet to see or hear of a demon that is not terrified of that or the mere mention of casting it into that furious lake of fire in the name of Jesus Christ. So the question does arise in many intelligent minds, how hot is hell and why are demons so scared of the place?

Let's take a logical view of things now as I try to explain.

Natural Fires

A cooking gas fire (which is natural gas that occurs in nature with crude oil) can burn as high as 300-400 degrees Celsius, which is definitely hotter than the regular fires that burn down a house. Interestingly, volcano fires, which have molten rocks in them, burn at 1,250 degrees Celsius.

These are the hottest natural fires on earth and man cannot do much better artificially. If you want to understand exactly how hot these fires are, then consider this; a pot of boiling water that can skin a man alive takes just a few minutes to boil over a cooking gas fire and has a temperature of only 100 degrees Celsius.

Nuclear Fires

Nuclear or thermonuclear fires, do not belong on earth, but out in the vast expanse of the universe. These are the fires that burn endlessly in the stars (suns are stars too). However, by his intelligence, man has discovered that using certain natural substances like hydrogen, uranium, and plutonium, he is able to recreate the fires of the stars and even harass the vast energy therein. Nations that possess this ability are commonly known as **nuclear powers** and they are very few in number.

The core of a nuclear reactor has a maximum temperature of just 300 degrees Celsius, but don't be fooled. The temperature in a nuclear reactor is very controlled and constantly being cooled by the inflow and outflow of water. The core of nuclear bombs, on the other hand, are beyond man's control.

Temperatures within a nuclear explosion can reach those in the interior of the sun, about 100,000,000 degrees Celsius, and produces a dazzling fireball.

On August 6, 1945, during the last days of World War II (1939-45), an American B-29 bomber dropped the world's first atomic bomb on the Japanese city of Hiroshima. The explosion destroyed 90 percent of the city and instantly killed 80,000 people; tens of thousands more would later die of exposure to radiation.

Native inhabitants of islands hundreds of miles away in the Pacific and Indian oceans swore that the sun rose and fell twice that day.

According to modern standards and technology, the bomb dropped on Hiroshima was a very small one. Interestingly, the sun which these bombs are compared to is a small star in a universe full of billions of stars, some of which are supergiants!

Rev. Ezekiel King

Hell Fire

The question we must now ask ourselves here is, if God created natural fires and nuclear fires to help man on earth and beautify the sky above his head, fires that, though so hot, have no effect on demons (and other spirit beings), what kind of fire did He create in hell that demons should fear it so much?

Personally, I have no idea, having never been to or seen the place before, a situation that will definitely remain so forever. However, the Bible, which calls the sun and stars beautiful and a blessing to man, portrays hell as a most terrible place where the fire and torment never ends. From experience and all I have heard, I know that whenever someone with authority attempts to cast a demon into hell, it cringes in terror and some demons have even been known to plead for mercy.

There is power in the name of Jesus Christ and God made this so for the good of mankind.

Rev. Ezekiel King

61. WHAT IS THE REFLECTION OF DEMONS IN MIRRORS?

In the minds of people with little knowledge of the supernatural, this question can take two different forms and we will answer both.

1. What is the reflection of demons that have taken human form?
2. What is the reflection of demons in their actual form?

One of the most popular ideas on this subject, which is based on the movie editing skills and trick photography abilities of Hollywood, is that when demons take human form they are generally stunning in looks; they are incredible beauties who do not age, or simply put, people of utter physical perfection; but if they have their back to a mirror there is no reflection!

Another popular theory here is that, though demons cannot be seen with the naked eyes when you take a picture of an area in which a demon is there is some sort of anomaly in the photo that can actually be seen.

Rev. Ezekiel King

While there is some truth in these two theories, they are not entirely correct, particularly the first. For one thing, demons cannot take human form. The best they can do is possess humans and lead them to do evil. As for aging, a human must age, whatever they do. That ageless vampire/demon in human body theory has no application outside a movie.

Personally, I have not had the opportunity to check the reflection of any possessed person in a mirror before, but going from the publication of Christian priests who lived in ages past, possessed people often have bizarre reflections in mirrors. One theory has it that the refection of this manner of people can even take the form of serpents, particularly in the face.

How about photography? While normal people cannot see or sense demons, it would appear that the photographic lens of cameras can capture their presence in certain ways. You need only do a quick search on the internet to find abundant proof of what I am saying. Too many people have reported seeing odd ghost-like shapes and appearances showing up in photos they have taken of odd places where nothing should be.

Things like this tend to occur mostly in houses, castles or any place with a long history of human inhabitation tampered by a vile sin such as murder or suicide. My advice to people who have this kind of experience would be not to linger in such places. Leave immediately and do not return.

62. CAN DEMONS HAVE SEX WITH PEOPLE?

Yes, they definitely can. In fact, there is an entire group/type of demons that attack humans that way precisely. They are known as sex demons.

Sex demons can be divided into three subcategories.

1. Incubus and Succubus
2. Spirit husbands and Spirit Wives
3. Marine Spirits

Regardless of subcategory, these are all demons that specialize in bringing humans down through sex. However, there is a slight difference in the way they operate.

Incubus and Succubus

This group of demons are also known collectively as Incubus demons. Incubus and succubus are the ancient names given to the male and female sex demons that sleeps with people randomly. An incubus is the male version of

Rev. Ezekiel King

this demon and it victimizes women, while the female version, which is a succubus, victimizes men.

Among several learned priests, saints and scholars of the Catholic Church who brought the activities of this particular class of sex demons to light "officially", the two men that stood out as pioneers were St. Augustine and King James of England and Scotland, author of the King James Version of the Holy Bible.

King James also shared this view and in his thesis titled Dæmonologie, he disproves the possibility of angelic beings ever being able to reproduce. He offered, instead, the suggestion that a demon could only impregnate a woman in two ways: the first was to steal the seed (sperm or semen) out of a dead man and then transfer it into a woman. The problem with this theory is that if a demon or any supernatural being for that matter could extract the sperm of a dead

Rev. Ezekiel King

man quickly enough after death, the
transportation of the warm, delicate
substance to a female host could
never be instant, resulting in it's
going cold and useless. King James
presented another theory here....
   *TOTAL DELIVERANCE
FROM SPIRIT HUSBAND AND
SPIRIT WIFE by Rev. Ezekiel King

The original names of these demons were Incubi and Succubi, but, with time, it became Incubus and Succubus.

After the public presentations of St. Augustine on the activities of these demons, due to the fear such fact caused, a lot of women thought to have been impregnated by demons were burnt alive throughout Christendom. So were many dead bodies.

Spirit Husband and Spirit Wives

271

Spirit husbands and spirit wives are sex demons as well. In fact, they are one and the same with the incubus and succubus demons. The only difference is that they come into people live to stay forever! They actually marry their victims and have children, all spiritually!

Marine Spirits

Marine spirits are female demons from the water world who possess women, particularly very beautiful women, and use them as sex tools to destroy men. The major weapons in use here is not just sex alone, but blinding good looks as well. A marine or water spirit aims to have illicit sexual affairs with as many different men as possible. They destroy each man's life systematically and completely and then move on to the next victim.

Of these three classes of demons, the most common are the first two. My book, ***Total Deliverance from Spirit Husband and Spirit Wife: Incubus and Succubus (Incubus Demons)*** will give you a wealth of knowledge in dealing with and gaining freedom from these sex demons.

Rev. Ezekiel King

273

63. CAN DEMONS TAMPER WITH UNBORN BABES?

Yes, they definitely can and they do it a lot more often than most people think. This is one of the most overlooked areas of demonic attacks I have ever come across and most religious leaders don't even know it exists, much less have a clue as to how to combat it.

When a woman becomes pregnant, all her thoughts, and even those of her husband, are towards antenatal and postnatal care. No one gives much thought to what demons can do to both the mother and the unborn child during that period.

Sadly, demons have identified people's ignorance in this area and stepped up their activities markedly, particularly over the last 100 years. The worst part is that their victims always have to suffer for life.

So what do these demons do exactly? Demons can alter the nature of an unborn child in different ways – physically, mentally, and psychologically – without the mother even realizing it. By the time that child is finally born, what you have is a very complex or abnormal child. The number of children born this way today is alarming,

Rev. Ezekiel King

and trust me when I say God does not give anyone such a terrible blessing.

Homosexuals, lesbians, hermaphrodites, intersex people, deformed babies, Siamese or conjoined twins, sadists, criminal minds, and many more. These are what you get when demons have tampered with the seed in a woman's womb. Forget medical or biological explanation, there is nothing normal in these births and only evil come of them. Evil is the work of demons and many don't even believe they exist.

In my next book, I intend to attack this issue and provide solutions for deliverance to everyone. You must all have life and live it in Jesus name.

Amen.

Rev. Ezekiel King

64. CAN YOU TALK TO A DEMON?

Although people cannot hear and see demons, supernatural beings that they are, they can hear and see humans loud and clear. Demons can even hear your thoughts. Whatever you do or say or plan to do or say, they already know. This is one way in which demons predict the future actions of people and plan ahead of them.

In reality, anyone that can speak or think in the words of any language can actually talk to a demon, but the problem would be knowing who you are talking to and getting answers to whatever you say.

Since ancient times, for one reason or the other, people have always wanted to speak directly to demons; sometimes they do this in a bid to set someone free. The medium often used is an Ouija board (also known as a spirit board). Those boards are very much around today and are mostly associated with occults and witchcraft. These are not things Christians should try, you do not need to.

The only thing Christians should be doing is getting rid of demons at all costs Stand and speak with authority in the name of Jesus and every demon shall bow because they

Rev. Ezekiel King

will hear you. Cast them out of your life and home and they will be gone for good.

For those curious minds still wondering where men of God and seers blessed with the divine gift of spiritual vision and awareness stand in this matter, the answer is that demons, like all supernatural beings, can communicate verbally and telepathically in different languages. And that is how "we speak with them and challenge them."

Rev. Ezekiel King

65. CAN DEMONS GIVE PROPHECY?

Yes, demons can give prophecies and have been doing so for ages! Demons give prophecies by two means: by means of their supernatural abilities and by their Special God-given ability. Yes, you hear correctly, "God given ability". Below, we explain each point further.

Supernatural Abilities

By means of their supernatural abilities, spirits of high order can give prophecies after a fashion and demons are no exception. Spirits of high order can read the minds (thoughts) of human beings and even see the darkest secrets and deeds of their lives in ways that defy logical explanation. By this key information alone, they can reveal amazing facts about a person's life, past, present, and future in a way that can be passed off as prophecies! People do not understand this strange phenomenon and have been falling victims to it for ages.

One good case study here is to be found in an incident that took place about 3,500 years ago and was recorded in the old testament of the Holy Bible. It involved

Rev. Ezekiel King

King Ahab of Israel who led God's children into sin through the worship of the demon-god Baal, thereby causing God great anger. Rather than interfere directly in the order of things on earth by striking the offending king dead, God led him into a war where he was killed. It is the way in which God did this that is important to us here. Read about it for yourself....

> *22 For three years there was no war between Aram and Israel. 2 But in the third year Jehoshaphat king of Judah went down to see the king of Israel. 3 The king of Israel had said to his officials, "Don't you know that Ramoth Gilead belongs to us and yet we are doing nothing to retake it from the king of Aram?"*
>
> *4 So he asked Jehoshaphat, "Will you go with me to fight against Ramoth Gilead?"*
>
> *Jehoshaphat replied to the king of Israel, "I am as you are, my people as your people, my horses as*

Rev. Ezekiel King

your horses." 5 But Jehoshaphat also said to the king of Israel, "First seek the counsel of the Lord."

6 So the king of Israel brought together the prophets—about four hundred men—and asked them, "Shall I go to war against Ramoth Gilead, or shall I refrain?"

"Go," they answered, "for the Lord will give it into the king's hand."

7 But Jehoshaphat asked, "Is there no longer a prophet of the Lord here whom we can inquire of?"

8 The king of Israel answered Jehoshaphat, "There is still one prophet through whom we can inquire of the Lord, but I hate him because he never prophesies anything good about me, but always bad. He is Micaiah son of Imlah."

"The king should not say such a thing," Jehoshaphat replied.

9 So the king of Israel called one of his officials and said, "Bring Micaiah son of Imlah at once."

10 Dressed in their royal robes, the king of Israel and Jehoshaphat king of Judah were sitting on their thrones at the threshing floor by the entrance of the gate of Samaria, with all the prophets prophesying before them. 11 Now Zedekiah son of Kenaanah had made iron horns and he declared, "This is what the Lord says: 'With these you will gore the Arameans until they are destroyed.'"

12 All the other prophets were prophesying the same thing. "Attack Ramoth Gilead and be victorious," they said, "for the Lord will give it into the king's hand."

13 The messenger who had gone to summon Micaiah said to him, "Look, the other prophets without exception are predicting success for

281

the king. Let your word agree with theirs, and speak favorably."

14 But Micaiah said, "As surely as the Lord lives, I can tell him only what the Lord tells me."

15 When he arrived, the king asked him, "Micaiah, shall we go to war against Ramoth Gilead, or not?"

"Attack and be victorious," he answered, "for the Lord will give it into the king's hand."

16 The king said to him, "How many times must I make you swear to tell me nothing but the truth in the name of the Lord?"

17 Then Micaiah answered, "I saw all Israel scattered on the hills like sheep without a shepherd, and the Lord said, 'These people have no master. Let each one go home in peace.'"

18 The king of Israel said to Jehoshaphat, "Didn't I tell you that he never prophesies anything good about me, but only bad?"

19 Micaiah continued, "Therefore hear the word of the Lord: I saw the Lord sitting on his throne with all the multitudes of heaven standing around him on his right and on his left. 20 And the Lord said, 'Who will entice Ahab into attacking Ramoth Gilead and going to his death there?'

"One suggested this, and another that. 21 Finally, a spirit came forward, stood before the Lord and said, 'I will entice him.'

22 "'By what means?' the Lord asked.

"'I will go out and be a deceiving spirit in the mouths of all his prophets,' he said.

"'You will succeed in enticing him,' said the Lord. 'Go and do it.'

283

Rev. Ezekiel King

23 "So now the Lord has put a deceiving spirit in the mouths of all these prophets of yours. The Lord has decreed disaster for you."

24 Then Zedekiah son of Kenaanah went up and slapped Micaiah in the face. "Which way did the spirit from[a] the Lord go when he went from me to speak to you?" he asked.

25 Micaiah replied, "You will find out on the day you go to hide in an inner room."

26 The king of Israel then ordered, "Take Micaiah and send him back to Amon the ruler of the city and to Joash the king's son 27 and say, 'This is what the king says: Put this fellow in prison and give him nothing but bread and water until I return safely.'"

28 Micaiah declared, "If you ever return safely, the Lord has not spoken through me." Then he added, "Mark my words, all you people!"

29 So the king of Israel and Jehoshaphat king of Judah went up to Ramoth Gilead. 30 The king of Israel said to Jehoshaphat, "I will enter the battle in disguise, but you wear your royal robes." So the king of Israel disguised himself and went into battle.

31 Now the king of Aram had ordered his thirty-two chariot commanders, "Do not fight with anyone, small or great, except the king of Israel." 32 When the chariot commanders saw Jehoshaphat, they thought, "Surely this is the king of Israel." So they turned to attack him, but when Jehoshaphat cried out, 33 the chariot commanders saw that he was not the king of Israel and stopped pursuing him.

34 But someone drew his bow at random and hit the king of Israel

Rev. Ezekiel King

between the sections of his armor.
The king told his chariot driver,
"Wheel around and get me out of the
fighting. I've been wounded." 35 All
day long the battle raged, and the
king was propped up in his chariot
facing the Arameans. The blood from
his wound ran onto the floor of the
chariot, and that evening he died. 36
As the sun was setting, a cry spread
through the army: "Every man to his
town. Every man to his land!"

37 So the king died and was
brought to Samaria, and they buried
him there. 38 They washed the
chariot at a pool in Samaria (where
the prostitutes bathed),[b] and the
dogs licked up his blood, as the word
of the Lord had declared.

39 As for the other events of
Ahab's reign, including all he did,
the palace he built and adorned with
ivory, and the cities he fortified, are
they not written in the book of the

Rev. Ezekiel King

annals of the kings of Israel? 40
Ahab rested with his ancestors. And
Ahaziah his son succeeded him as
king.

1 Kings 22 New
International Version (NIV)

As we have seen, a single spirit (angel) made more than 400 prophets give misleading information to a king. But then one might wonder if these prophets of God lied. Not at all. They said exactly what God wanted them to say and God, who is truth itself, laid open the entire setup before King Ahab through another prophet, Micaiah, thereby vindicating his holy name of any evil.

Bottom line, King Ahab was told precisely the truth but did not listen. He went to war and was killed. All this was caused by an angel of God directly.

Demons are fallen angels, spirits of high order, and can defiantly do things like this, but in a very evil way. Demons possess people and make them utter a clever mixture of lies and half-truth that can pass for prophecies when spoken in a mysterious manner, etc. False prophets, false priests and false pastors, witches, mediums, etc., these are their agents. Even mad people, the violently possessed, have been known to give prophecies that seem true in crazy ways.

Special God-Given Abilities

In that way that God created humans with different unique talents and abilities so also did He create angelic beings. There are some angelic beings with the unique ability to read the intricate trends of life, both the spiritual and physical aspect, far into the future. These angels or spirits are specifically known as the "**Spirits of prophecy**" and their sole duty is to act as a kind of liaison between God and mankind.

The spirits of prophecy are very few, they stand in the presence of God and are completely holy. They choose and form bonds with certain people of pure nature in whom they can dwell comfortably and, through them, channel the word and the will of God to the world, live and direct. These people become known as prophets of God and must maintain a life of extreme purity.

Some of these angels (or spirits) of prophecy, where with Satan in the day he rebelled against God and was cast out of heaven. From then on, they became **Demons of False Prophecy,** beings of utter evil.

In the Bible Book of Acts, we have a very good example of what a demon of false prophecy is really like…

16 Once when we were going to the place of prayer, we were met by a female slave who had a spirit by which she predicted the future. She earned a great deal of money for her owners by fortune-telling. 17 She followed Paul and the rest of us, shouting, "These men are servants of the Most High God, who are telling you the way to be saved." 18 She kept this up for many days. Finally, Paul became so annoyed that he turned around and said to the spirit, "In the name of Jesus Christ I command you to come out of her!" At that moment the spirit left her.

19 When her owners realized that their hope of making money was

289

gone, they seized Paul and Silas and dragged them into the marketplace to face the authorities. 20 They brought them before the magistrates and said, "These men are Jews, and are throwing our city into an uproar 21 by advocating customs unlawful for us Romans to accept or practice."
Acts 16:16-21 New International Version (NIV)

What we have here is a little girl possessed by a genuine demonic spirit of prophecy that has bowed unconditionally to the superior authority and power of the living God in the apostles.

The majority of the powerful false prophets, fake pastors who- are church founders and leaders today are filled with this evil demon of prophecy., and let's not forget the priest of pagan gods, mediums, and fortune tellers.

How Does One Tell Between a True and False Prophet?

Rev. Ezekiel King

Only God and those whom He blesses with some certain divine gifts can identify the manner of spirit in operation within a person as was evident in the way in which the Apostle Paul identified the evil spirit in the girl. The only way ordinary people can figure things like this out is to look towards a tendency to tolerate sin. The holy spirit of prophecy from God does not tolerate sin in any manner, whereas demonic spirits of prophecy actually encourage it.

If you ever become suspicious of the origin of a prophet's power, the following are some of the signs to look out for...

1. **Payment for Services**: Any prophet who, either directly or indirectly, asks for payment in any way before or after giving a prophecy is filled with unclean spirits. This can take a wide range of forms; compulsory donation is one. However, there are cases where a good prophet is surrounded by vile people who take those donations. Still, such a setup never lasts long. God's blessings are free to humans!

2. **Flamboyance**: Is the prophet flamboyant with wealth? Most prophets today are, but when they

Rev. Ezekiel King

overdo it to a shameful extent that is pride and God hates pride. The Holy Spirit will never be in such a person.

3. **Controversy**: Is a prophet constantly getting caught up in the controversy of inaccurate prophecies and having to clarify himself? That's a demon and its half-truths and lies at work.

4. **Fornication & Adultery**: This is a great sin. Only false prophets can do this and still retain their power and position, spiritually and physically.

5. **Fraud**: This is a very common sin in many churches today, but it is tantamount to theft. Only false prophets do this and still hold any form of power.

6. **The Quest for Fame**: Where you find a prophet that will say or do anything to become famous or attract fame, that is a false prophet in action. He will often get caught up in embarrassing controversies because of that.

Rev. Ezekiel King

7. **Self-Glorification**: This is where a prophet takes the glory for the miracles and wonders he performs. That is a demon at work.

8. **Magic**: Only false prophets perform acts akin to magic.

9. **Association with Demons**: Most false prophets are founders or leaders of seemingly legitimate churches and so go through great length to hide their connection to demons and pagan gods who are the source of their power. Still, such a secret always has a way of leaking out.

   In the month of May 2019, members of a big church in Ghana, West Africa, were rocked when a witch-doctor walked right into the church in full session to demand that the prophet/founder returns the power he was given. The witch-doctor, Kwaku Bonsam, operates from an old shrine located in the tiny village of Sa-Peiman, eastern Ghana. He calls his god *Kofi-Kofi* and boasts of being the source of the supernatural powers used by more than 1,700

Rev. Ezekiel King

prophets and pastors around the world. He has a reputation for clashing with some of the most popular prophets and church founders in Africa.

10. **Lack of Love for the Poor**: Jesus loved the poor and needy when he was on earth and declared that the kingdom of heaven is for them. Any prophet or pastor that shuts out this particular group of people is not of God.

The signs are endless and no false prophet or pastor can hide them all. Where any one of these sins mentioned above is present in the life of a true prophet of God, the Holy Spirit will depart and that person will become very ordinary. God may tolerate and forgive sin all the time in ordinary people, but with his prophets, He is very strict for his Spirit and name is in them. One false word or prophecy, one false move, and they are done...

> 7 "'*When any of the Israelites*
> *or any foreigner residing in Israel*
> *separate themselves from me and set*

Rev. Ezekiel King

up idols in their hearts and put a wicked stumbling block before their faces and then go to a prophet to inquire of me, I the Lord will answer them myself. 8 I will set my face against them and make them an example and a byword. I will remove them from my people. Then you will know that I am the Lord.

9 "'And if the prophet is enticed to utter a prophecy, I the Lord have enticed that prophet, and I will stretch out my hand against him and destroy him from among my people Israel. 10 They will bear their guilt—the prophet will be as guilty as the one who consults him.

Ezekiel 14: 14:7-10 New International Version (NIV)

A holy prophet is but a messenger before God and cannot add or remove a single word from that which God has put in his mouth. If he does, he will lose that gift and

Rev. Ezekiel King

his destiny, both. Hence, no matter how many prophets of God one visits with a problem the answer is always the same, whether good or bad. But visit false prophets and the answer will change constantly. In most cases, the half-truths and lies will simply become too confusing.

Only false prophets sin, over and over again and still retain their power and position without any visible problems. This is so because that power is not of God.

66. WHAT KIND OF PRAYERS DRIVE OUT DEMONS

Normal prayers do not drive out demons at all. In fact, the presence of that demon or demons in the victim's body or life will do everything to hinder that prayer from getting to God and frustrate everyone involved in that deliverance attempt. This is a lot like trying to kill a huge tree by cutting off the leaves.

The only prayer that works against demons is that of authority and finality. A command to leave and never return. Let's see how the Apostle Paul does it...

> *16 Once when we were going to the place of prayer, we were met by a female slave who had a spirit by which she predicted the future. She earned a great deal of money for her owners by fortune-telling. 17 She followed Paul and the rest of us, shouting, "These men are servants of the Most High God, who are telling*

Rev. Ezekiel King

you the way to be saved." 18 She kept
this up for many days. Finally, Paul
became so annoyed that he turned
around and said to the spirit, "In the
name of Jesus Christ I command you
to come out of her!" At that moment
the spirit left her.

Acts 16:16-40 New
International Version (NIV)

And there you have it… a direct command! It is
called casting out demons and every Christina has the
authority to do that in the name of Jesus Christ.

Lack of faith and sin are the only hindrance in the
way of Christians who wish to cast out a demon. If you
don't suffer from the first, then fast and pray to fix the
second after which you may confront any demon in Jesus
name and be free!

Also See Chapter 20: **Who Can Cast out Demons**?

Rev. Ezekiel King

67. ARE THERE MALE AND FEMALE DEMONS?

Now here is a very complicated question to answer, but answer it we will.

Almost every living thing in the physical world, humans included, have male and female versions of themselves. This is so because God made it that way that they may **be fruitful and multiply over the surface of the earth** (*Creation vs Evolution* by Rev. Ezekiel King).

That divine blessing "**Be fruitful and multiply**" was given only to creatures of the physical world (the earth) not creatures of the supernatural world. Supernatural beings were not created to multiply and so do not have male and female versions of themselves – God did not make them so.

If a gender must be chosen for clarity's sake, God himself and all the angelic beings of heaven would come firmly under the masculine gender. Throughout the bible they are all referred to as "HE" and in the day God created man in his own image and likeness, God created him a **male**. It was only later that God created a woman to be a

299

helper and **companion** onto the man, and thus did females/women come to exist.

Do you need more proof that God and the angelic creatures of heaven are "male"? Ardent readers of the Bible can help you out. They will tell you that, all through the Bible, these holy beings of heave rarely associated with or appeared to women directly. God, in particular, never did. He has an evasion to contact with women and in the day He dwelt in a tent among the Israelites He made it perfectly clear severally that women could not come near that tent in any manner and even men who did must not have slept with a woman for at least 3 days. Even till this day, there are prophets of God I know who sleep in a different room from their wives just to maintain a high level of holiness before God.

Another interesting thing of note is that of all the people to ever walk the earth, the only three who never died because God took them directly to heaven to be with him are Enoch, Moses, and Elijah, all are men!

At this point, therefore, you will understand better when I say that demons, fallen angels that they are, have no male and female version of themselves. However, there is a particular group of demons that use sex as a weapon against mankind. They are known as sex demons and some of them are horrible perversions of evil that take on male and female forms to lust after humanity. Below is a basic breakdown of this group of demons.

- **Incubus**: Male sex demon that has sex with women.
- **Succubus**: Female sex demon that has sex with men.
- **Marine Spirits**: Very powerful female sex demons that possess lovely women and use them as sex tools against men. Some of these demons have been worshipped as goddesses in some lands for ages!

Also See Chapter 62: Can Demons Have Sex with People?

68. WHERE DO DEMONS LIVE?

The science of astronomy has finally made people aware that there are billions of worlds (planets) in the vast universes, but none has any concrete traces of life except the earth on which we live. The Bible has been telling us all this since ancient times, but it has always been telling us something else – that ever since they were cast out of heaven, demons have chosen the earth as a new home and main base for their evil operations.

> *2 Again there was a day when the sons of God came to present themselves before the Lord, and Satan came also among them to present himself before the Lord. 2 And the Lord said to Satan, "From where do you come?"*
>
> *Satan answered the Lord and said, "From going to and fro on the earth, and from walking back and forth on it."*

Rev. Ezekiel King

Job 2 New King James Version (NKJV)

The question titling this chapter may now be rephrased thus; where on earth do demons live?

Their homes are right there in unique locations all over the earth, but we just don't see them because they are on a different level of the existence... the supernatural (spiritual).

On mountaintops, hilltops, in caves, in forest and by huge trees, in wastelands/deserts, in water (the seas, rivers, streams), at waterfalls, crossroads, etc., demons have had their homes in places like these for ages and it may interest you to know that people have been building pagan shrines, temples, idols, and alters in all these places for thousands of years, worshiping and offering sacrifices to mysterious spirits they don't really know,

Demons of lower and mid-level authority and power wander aimlessly over the earth and can live almost anywhere, but the most powerful demons of high authority, such as Satan, rule over "kingdoms" or "territories", situated beneath water (seas, rivers, streams, lakes), beneath the surface of the earth, and in the sky. For

Rev. Ezekiel King

example, marine spirits are female demons of the water kingdom who, in many lands, have been portrayed and worshiped in riverside shrines as spiritual mermaids of great power.

Man is a curious creature and, since ancient times, has created idols and pagan places of worship wherever strange occurrences or supernatural activities of any sort are noticed, but does not understand that the same place is exactly where demons live.

Rev. Ezekiel King

69. FULL LIST OF DEMONIC ACTIVITIES

The following may help in highlighting your need to be released from demonic possession, oppression or bondage.

1. The unexplainable urge to abuse people or animals;

2. Sexual immorality and perversion (indulgence in homosexuality, lesbianism, molestation, sexual immorality, etc.);

3. Psychological disorders (multiple and split personalities, voice changes, paranoia, etc.);

4. The compulsion/urge to abuse your body (alcohol, drugs, gluttony, abuse or of other substances or their misuse, too many tattoos, etc.);

Rev. Ezekiel King

5. Physical disorders may or may not be demonic in origin (Matthew 9:32, 33);

6. Looking for spiritual knowledge through False or Eastern religions groups (Hinduism TM, Yoga, Buddhism, etc.);

7. Lack of joy or freedom in the Lord God Almighty (spiritual bondage).

8. Involvement in shrines or occult practices (witchcraft, magic, fortune-telling, Divination, Satanism, etc.);

9. Mental distress or insanity (anxiety, anger, fear, disorientation, confusion, etc.).

10. Constant refusal or inability to repent of sins, even with full awareness (rebellion).

70. OTHER GENERAL BIBLE VERSE ABOUT DEMONS

Below are some other Bible verses about demons that may enlighten you even further on their nature and activities.

- You believe that there is one God. Good! Even demons believe that and shudder. (James 2:19

- Submit yourselves, then, to God. Resist the devil, and he will flee from you (James 4:7).

- They must no longer offer any of their sacrifices to the goat idols to whom they prostitute themselves. This is to be a lasting ordinance for them and for the generations to come.' (Leviticus 17:7)

- Whenever the impure spirits saw him, they fell down before him and cried out, "You are the Son of God." (Mark 3:11)

Rev. Ezekiel King

- He replied, "This kind can come out only by prayer." (Mark 9:29)

- Jesus called his twelve disciples to him and gave them authority to drive out impure spirits and to heal every disease and sickness. (Matthew 10:1)

- Be alert and of sober mind. Your enemy the devil prowls around like a roaring lion looking for someone to devour. (1 Peter 5:8)

- 4 For if God did not spare angels when they sinned, but sent them to hell, putting them in chains of darkness to be held for judgment; (2 Peter 2:4)

- Then it goes and takes with it seven other spirits more wicked than itself, and they go in and live there. And the final condition of that person is worse than the first. That is how it will be with this wicked generation." (Matthew 12:45)

Rev. Ezekiel King

- 41 "Then he will say to those on his left, 'Depart from me, you who are cursed, into the eternal fire prepared for the devil and his angels. (Matthew 25:41)

- 1 The fifth angel sounded his trumpet, and I saw a star that had fallen from the sky to the earth. The star was given the key to the shaft of the Abyss. 2 When he opened the Abyss, smoke rose from it like the smoke from a gigantic furnace. The sun and sky were darkened by the smoke from the Abyss. 3 And out of the smoke locusts came down on the earth and were given power like that of scorpions of the earth. 4 They were told not to harm the grass of the earth or any plant or tree, but only those people who did not have the seal of God on their foreheads. 5 They were not allowed to kill them but only to torture them for five months. And the agony they suffered was like that of the sting of a scorpion when it strikes. 6 During those days, people will seek death but will not find

309

it; they will long to die, but death will elude them. 7 The locusts looked like horses prepared for battle. On their heads they wore something like crowns of gold, and their faces resembled human faces (Revelation 9:1-7)

A FINAL WORD TO ALL

If you are agnostic or simply refuse to believe in the existence, goals and evil cunning of demons, there isn't much I can say or do to help you at this point.

Parents, guardians, are any of your children or wards being vile in behavior? Before you pick up the stick to hit the child or even blame them, stop to consider that there may be an external influence at work in them... demons. The irony of this situation is that the more you beat or punish a sinful child under the influence of a demon, the more that child will rebel against you.

People with cheating partners are not left out. Fornication and adultery are huge sins. Though mankind is prone to sins like these, demons lurking in a person or meddling in their lives can be the cause or even escalate the problem. Before you attack or dump that cheating spouse, try to figure out the real origin of the problem and fix it. The same is the case with offending relatives, friends, colleagues and neighbors; demons love nothing more than to put enmity between two close people.

Have you noticed a series of ill-luck or misfortune in your life? Or is it just persistent ill-health that defy

Rev. Ezekiel King

medical explanations and cure? You are most likely up against a demon.

Whatever the case, read through this book, isolate your problem and the demon causing it, then get rid of both and be free.

May God Almighty Bless and Protect You Forever. Amen!

Rev. Ezekiel King

THE END

Rev. Ezekiel King

OTHER BOOKS BY THE AUTHOR

Below is a full list of other published books by this author, George Kennedy.

1. **Creation vs Evolution: Scientific and Spiritual Proof That Life was Designed.**
2. **How to Pray to God and Always be heard: Turning**
3. **Total Deliverance from Spiritual Husband and Spiritual Wife, Incubus and Succubus, Incubus demon**

To find direct links to purchase any of these book on your favorite bookstore please visit the author's book page on the publisher's website.

Rev. Ezekiel King's Books Page

https://www.kingreads.com/tag/author-ezekiel-kings-books/

Rev. Ezekiel King

ABOUT THE AUTHOR

Rev. Ezekiel King is a former co-founder of Holy Ghost Prayer and Healing Ministry (1994-99). He is currently a humble worker of Christ Holy Church International.

Taking God's word to all the people and nations of the world is his goal.

315

Rev. Ezekiel King

ABOUT THE PUBLISHER

Kingreads is a book publishing and promotions team that works strictly with talented authors and individuals with good books to publish.

Fid more books on our website: **kingreads.com**

View Our author list:

https://www.kingreads.com/authors/

Find more Kindle Unlimited Books:

https://www.kingreads.com/kindle-unlimited-books-kingreads/

Kingreads: *We publish only the beset books.*

Rev. Ezekiel King

NOTES

317

Rev. Ezekiel King

NOTE